Careers in Focus

COSMETOLOGY

FOURTH EDITION

Ferguson
An imprint of Infobase Publishing

Careers in Focus: Cosmetology, Fourth Edition

Copyright © 2008 by Infobase Publishing

Ferguson
An imprint of Infobase Publishing
132 West 31st Street
New York NY 10001

Library of Congress Cataloging-in-Publication Data

Careers in focus. Cosmetology. — 4th ed.
        p. cm.
    Includes bibliographical references and index.
    ISBN-13: 978-0-8160-7271-2
    ISBN-10: 0-8160-7271-X
    1. Beauty culture—Vocational guidance—United States. I. J.G. Ferguson Publishing Company.
    TT958.C367 2008
    646.7'2023—dc22
                                              2007038383

Ferguson books are available at special discounts when purchased in bulk quantities for businesses, associations, institutions, or sales promotions. Please call our Special Sales Department in New York at (212) 967-8800 or (800) 322-8755.

You can find Ferguson on the World Wide Web at http://www.fergpubco.com

Text design by David Strelecky
Cover design by Salvatore Luongo

Printed in the United States of America

MP MSRF 10 9 8 7 6 5 4 3 2

This book is printed on acid-free paper.

Table of Contents

Introduction

From a new summer 'do to a milk-and-honey facial, from a leg waxing to an eyebrow plucking, cosmetologists provide a wide range of beauty and health services. Back when a shave and a haircut cost two bits, men spent their lunch hours relaxing in hydraulic barber chairs for hot, aromatic shaves. Meanwhile, women got their hair done in beauty salons, while also indulging in occasional manicures and facials. This attention to skin care and hair care is no longer regarded as an indulgence; as a matter of fact, some doctors are beginning to prescribe spa treatments for their patients. The cosmetology industry is at the forefront of new attitudes regarding mind-body awareness, relaxation techniques, nutrition, and spirituality. Now, men and women frequent the same salons, paying the same kind of attention to their hairstyles and appearance. Spas, which were considered the domain of rich old women for most of the 20th century, have become vacation spots of choice for men and women, young and old. Because of its stability, growth potential, and financial security, cosmetology has been highly ranked in recent career surveys by *Money, Women's World,* and the U.S. Bureau of Labor Statistics.

Cosmetologists work in many different settings; they may rent a chair in a local hairstyling salon or body-wrap spa guests at a tropical resort. Cosmetologists with experience in massage, facials, nail care, and hydrotherapy are finding jobs in the many day spas that are cropping up across the country. To compete, hair and nail salons are expanding to include additional rooms for face and body treatments. Fitness centers are also expanding their lines of service and are hiring massage therapists and spa attendants. New treatments, such as aromatherapy, and new products, such as herb-based, chemical-free cosmetics, require the industry to constantly change, adapting to trends and attitudes. But cosmetologists aren't limited to the spa and beauty salon. A variety of jobs are available in the film and television industries, the fashion industry, and at recreational parks, cosmetology schools, funeral homes, and health clubs.

Cosmetologists who have finished training and have received a state license to practice usually start in entry-level positions in salons. These positions might include floor sweeping, shampooing clients' hair, making appointments, ordering supplies, and performing other tasks. Gradually, new cosmetologists take on more responsibilities and have more direct client contact, starting with simple haircuts and styling. With more on-the-job experience they do more complicated haircuts and styles, perms, and hair coloring while building a client base.

Another popular alternative for cosmetologists is self-employment. Some freelance hair and makeup designers work with photographers, modeling agencies, film production companies, theaters, or television studios. Some open their own salons or rent a station in an established salon.

Because so many cosmetologists seek self-employment, there is a great deal of mobility within the industry. There are also a number of specialties within cosmetology. In hairstyling alone, cosmetologists can specialize in cuts, color, or perms. They may also become makeup artists, nail technicians, electrologists, image consultants, or developers and marketers of beauty products. According to the *Occupational Outlook Handbook,* there are 670,000 barbers, hairstylists, and cosmetologists; 60,000 manicurists and pedicurists; 30,000 skin care specialists; and 27,000 shampooers employed in the United States.

The cosmetology industry also includes people working in other career fields, such as health care (surgeons, dermatologists, surgical aides), the film industry (hair and makeup artists and special effects artists), advertising, retail sales, fitness, and management. Magazine, newspaper, and Web publishing offer opportunities for full-time and consultant cosmetology experts. There are a variety of jobs available in the manufacturing of beauty and personal care products (such as cosmetics, hair care products, skin care products, and toiletries), including chemical scientists, technicians, packaging designers and engineers, advertising and marketing professionals, sales and distribution personnel, and production workers.

Do an Internet search for "beauty salons" in your area and you'll see how much the industry is growing—you're likely to find a long list of salons. Day spas are also opening up across the country, and salons are expanding to include more spa services such as body wraps and massage. Hotels and resorts are adding salons, spas, and fitness centers to their facilities. The clientele of spas and salons has expanded to include men. Many skin care lines carry products for men, and cosmetic surgery is gaining wider acceptance among both men and women.

Those in the cosmetology industry, through such professional organizations as the National Accrediting Commission of Cosmetology Arts and Sciences and the Cosmetology Advancement Foundation, are making efforts to educate people about the varied career options within the industry. Due to the growing number of salons and the mobility within the industry, these cosmetology associations are actively recruiting people to meet the industry's high demand for workers.

The U.S. Department of Labor projects average growth for cosmetologists, hairdressers, and hairstylists through 2014. The number of barbershops is declining, but trained barbers should not have difficulty finding jobs because of the lack of qualified applicants. Employment for manicurists, pedicurists, and skin care specialists is expected to grow faster than the average for all occupations as a result of the growth of spas and nail salons. Overall, the high rate of turnover in the cosmetology field and the continuing demand for services should create plenty of opportunities.

Each article in *Careers in Focus: Cosmetology* discusses a particular cosmetology-related career in detail. The articles appear in Ferguson's *Encyclopedia of Careers and Vocational Guidance* but have been updated and revised with the latest information from the U.S. Department of Labor, professional organizations, and other sources. The following paragraphs detail the sections and features that appear in the book.

The **Quick Facts** section provides a brief summary of the career including recommended school subjects, personal skills, work environment, minimum educational requirements, salary ranges, certification or licensing requirements, and employment outlook. This section also provides acronyms and identification numbers for the following government classification indexes: the *Dictionary of Occupational Titles* (DOT), the *Guide for Occupational Exploration* (GOE), the National Occupational Classification (NOC) Index, and the Occupational Information Network (O*NET)-Standard Occupational Classification System (SOC) index. The DOT, GOE, and O*NET-SOC indexes have been created by the U.S. government; the NOC index is Canada's career-classification system. Readers can use the identification numbers listed in the Quick Facts section to access further information about a career. Print editions of the DOT (*Dictionary of Occupational Titles*. Indianapolis, Ind.: JIST Works, 1991) and GOE (*Guide for Occupational Exploration*. Indianapolis, Ind.: JIST Works, 2001) are available at libraries. Electronic versions of the NOC (http://www23.hrdc-drhc.gc.ca) and O*NET-SOC (http://online.onetcenter.org) are available on the Internet. When no DOT, GOE, NOC, or O*NET-SOC numbers are present, this means that the U.S. Department of Labor or Human Resources Development Canada have not created a numerical designation for this career. In this instance, you will see the acronym "N/A," or not available.

The **Overview** section is a brief introductory description of the duties and responsibilities involved in this career. Oftentimes, a career may have a variety of job titles. When this is the case, alternative career titles are presented.

The **History** section describes the history of the particular job as it relates to the overall development of its industry or field.

The **Job** describes the primary and secondary duties of the job.

Requirements discusses high school and postsecondary education and training requirements, any certification or licensing that is necessary, and other personal requirements for success in the job.

Exploring offers suggestions on how to gain experience in or knowledge of the particular job before making a firm educational and financial commitment. The focus is on what can be done while still in high school (or in the early years of college) to gain a better understanding of the job.

The **Employers** section gives an overview of typical places of employment for the job.

Starting Out discusses the best ways to land that first job, be it through the college career services office, newspaper ads, Internet employment sites, or personal contact.

The **Advancement** section describes what kind of career path to expect from the job and how to get there.

Earnings lists salary ranges and describes the typical fringe benefits.

The **Work Environment** section describes the typical surroundings and conditions of employment—whether indoors or outdoors, noisy or quiet, social or independent. Also discussed are typical hours worked, any seasonal fluctuations, and the stresses and strains of the job.

The **Outlook** section summarizes the job in terms of the general economy and industry projections. For the most part, Outlook information is obtained from the U.S. Bureau of Labor Statistics and is supplemented by information taken from professional associations. Job growth terms follow those used in the *Occupational Outlook Handbook*. Growth described as "much faster than the average" means an increase of 27 percent or more. Growth described as "faster than the average" means an increase of 18 to 26 percent. Growth described as "about as fast as the average" means an increase of 9 to 17 percent. Growth described as "more slowly than the average" means an increase of 0 to 8 percent. "Decline" means a decrease by any amount.

Each article ends with **For More Information,** which lists organizations that provide information on training, education, internships, scholarships, and job placement.

Careers in Focus: Cosmetology also includes photographs, informative sidebars, and interviews with professionals in the field.

Aromatherapists

OVERVIEW

Aromatherapists are health care specialists who use essential plant oils to promote health in their clients. Essential oils are highly concentrated substances that give plants their fragrance. These substances are extracted from various parts of aromatic plants, such as roots, woods, seeds, fruits, leaves, and flowers. Only about 5 percent of all types of plants are used for their essential oils.

Since the early 20th century, the professions of cosmetology, medicine, and psychology have rediscovered the healing powers of essential oils that were known to earlier civilizations. Scientific studies show that inhaling the fragrance of certain essential oils has physiological and psychological effects on the brain. Aromatherapists study the oils and their effects on individuals. They use this knowledge to help improve their clients' quality of life.

Most aromatherapists are licensed in other areas of health care or body care, using aromatherapy as a supplementary tool in their licensed profession. Among these licensed professionals are beauticians, chiropractors, cosmeticians, massage therapists, medical doctors, naturopathic doctors, nurse practitioners, and nurses. A few individuals who specialize in aromatherapy work as chemists, educators, or authors. A very few grow plants for the distillation of essential oils, become consultants, or start their own lines of aromatherapy products.

QUICK FACTS

School Subjects
Biology
Chemistry
English

Personal Skills
Helping/teaching
Technical/scientific

Work Environment
Primarily indoors
Primarily one location

Minimum Education Level
Some postsecondary
training

Salary Range
$12,920 to $45,000 to
$80,000+

Certification or Licensing
Voluntary

Outlook
Faster than the average

DOT
N/A

GOE
N/A

NOC
3232

O*NET-SOC
N/A

HISTORY

Humanity's use of fragrance probably began long before recorded history. Anthropologists think that primitive people burned gums and resin as incense. Throughout history, civilizations have used essential oils for many purposes—including healing. As an art and science, aromatherapy finds its roots in ancient cultures, dating back 4,000 to 5,000 years. Early Egyptians are often credited with being the first to make an art of the use of essential oils. They used myrrh and frankincense (fragrant resins from trees) in their daily rituals. However, other early cultures also used essential oils. In ancient Africa, people discovered that certain plants provided protection from the sun when they were rubbed on the skin. Chinese, Indian, Persian, and other African cultures used plant oils for incense burning, cooking, cosmetics, mummifying, bathing, perfumery, meditating, and healing.

In the spas of ancient Rome, oils were used in public baths and were applied during massages. The knowledge of oils went along with the spread of Roman culture. Europeans used oils during medieval times to fight disease. During the Middle Ages, the appearance of chemistry and the improvement of distillation helped simplify the process of extracting essential oils from plants. This opened the door to oil trading, which spread the new practices to more people and places.

Until the 19th century, when science began to introduce other medicines, Europeans used essential oils both as perfumes and for medicinal purposes. With the growth of newer medical practices, doctors began to choose modern medicine over the tradition of oils. It was not until the 20th century that several individuals "rediscovered" the healing power of essential oils. Once again the use of oils was integrated into Western culture.

In 1928, the French perfumer and chemist, René-Maurice Gattefossé, experienced the healing power of essential oils. When he severely burned his hand, he stuck it into the nearest liquid, which happened to be lavender oil. He was surprised how quickly the hand healed. His experience caused him to become interested in the therapeutic use of essential oils. It was Gattefossé who coined the term *aromatherapy.*

Dr. Jean Valnet, a French physician, was the first to reintegrate essential oils into Western medical practice. Dr. Valnet served as an army surgeon during World War II. Inspired by the work of Gattefossé, he used essential oils to treat the soldiers' burns and wounds. He also successfully treated psychiatric problems with fragrances.

Marguerite Maury, an Austrian biochemist, was also influenced by the work of Gattefossé. She integrated the use of essential oils into cosmetics.

In 1977, Robert Tisserand, an expert in aromatherapy, wrote *The Art of Aromatherapy*. Tisserand was strongly influenced by the work of both Gattefossé and Valnet. His book caught the interest of the American public and made a major contribution to the growth of aromatherapy in this country.

The Western world has rediscovered the uses of essential oils and fragrances through the work of people like Valnet, Maury, and Tisserand. In France, aromatherapy is practiced by medical doctors. Conventional and alternative medicine practitioners in England, Australia, Sweden, Japan, the United States, and other parts of the world are recognizing and utilizing the healing power of essential oils. The world is reawakening to the healing and life-enhancing capabilities of aromatherapy.

THE JOB

Whether aromatherapists work primarily as beauticians, chiropractors, massage therapists, or doctors, they must possess a strong working knowledge of aromatherapy as a science and an art. They need to understand the components and healing benefits of many essential oils. The quality of essential oils varies greatly depending on the plant, where it is grown, the conditions under which it is grown, and other factors. As a result, aromatherapists must be very careful about choosing the sources from which their oils come. Pure, high-quality, therapeutic-grade oils are essential to good aromatherapy. Aromatherapists must even know the differences between the oils of different species of the same plant. Essential oils are very powerful because of their high concentration. It may take well over 100 pounds of plant material to produce just one pound of essential oil.

Because of the powerful concentration of essential oils, aromatherapists use great care in diluting them and in adding them to what are called carrier oils. These are most often high-quality vegetable oils, such as almond, olive, or sesame. Unlike essential oils, carrier oils are fixed, rather than volatile. A small amount of an essential oil is blended into the carrier oil, which "carries" it across the body. Aromatherapists are especially careful when the oils are to be applied to a client's skin or put into a bath. In addition, aromatherapists must know how different essential oils work together because they are often combined to achieve certain results.

Aromatherapists need to know much more than what oils to use. They use the essential oils in three types of aromatherapy: cosmetic, massage, and olfactory. Aromatherapists have to know the differences among the types of therapy. They must decide which type or combination of types to use in a particular situation, and they must be skilled in each type.

Aromatherapists must know how the body, mind, and emotions work together. For example, a client who complains of muscle tension may need physical relief. A massage with relaxing oils that the skin soaks in will relax the client. However, aromatherapists are able to take this treatment a step further. They consider the underlying causes of the condition. Why is the client feeling tense? Is it stress? Anxiety? Strong emotion? Massage therapists who are trained in aromatherapy may inquire about the client's life in order to pinpoint the source of the tension. Once the source is identified, aromatherapists utilize specific oils to produce a certain emotional effect in the client. When the scents of these oils are inhaled, they create a response within the entire body. The oils may be added to a bath or a compress that is applied to the body. A compress is a towel soaked in water that has a bit of an essential oil added to it. An aroma may take the client back to happier times, as a reminder of warmth, comfort, and contentment.

An aromatherapist's client may have skin problems due to stress. The aromatherapist may use certain essential oils to help both the skin condition on the surface and the underlying emotional source of the problem. This might be accomplished through olfactory aromatherapy—the inhalation of the oil vapors.

In a hospital, nursing home, or hospice setting, an aromatherapist might choose essential oils that help relieve stress. In England, hospital nursing staffs utilize essential oil massage. This type of therapy has been shown to relieve pain and induce sleep. Essential oil massage has proven effective in relieving the stress that patients experience with general illness, surgery, terminal cancer, and AIDS. Aromatherapists emphasize that these treatments are supplementary and enhancing to medical care—they do not replace medical treatment.

No two clients' problems are the same, and neither are the remedies for those problems. Each client must be treated as an individual. During the first visit, aromatherapists usually take a careful client history. Aromatherapists must listen carefully both for things their clients say and for things they don't say. Aromatherapists need to know if a client is taking any medicine or using any natural healing substances, such as herbs. They must understand the properties of the essential oils and how they might interact with any other treatment the client is using. Next, they use the information gathered from the client interview to determine the proper essential oils and the appropriate amounts to blend to serve the client's particular needs.

Aromatherapists are employed in a number of different work environments. Those connected to the beauty industry may work in salons, spas, or hotel resorts, incorporating aromatherapy into facial care, body care, and hair care. In the health care field, many professionals are turning to alternative approaches to care, and some conventional medical practitioners are beginning to implement more holistic approaches. As a result, a growing number of aromatherapists work in the offices of other health care specialists, where their aromatherapy treatments complement the other therapies used. Aromatherapists often give seminars, teach, or serve as consultants. Some who become experts on essential oils buy farms to grow plants for the oils, create their own lines of aromatherapy products, or sell essential oils to other aromatherapists.

REQUIREMENTS

High School
If you are interested in working with aromatherapy, begin in high school by building up your knowledge of the human body's systems. Biology, anatomy, and physiology will help lay the foundation for a career in aromatherapy. Chemistry courses will familiarize you with laboratory procedures. Aromatherapists need to have an understanding of mixtures and the care involved in using powerful essential oils. Chemistry can help you gain the experience you need to handle delicate or volatile substances. It will also familiarize you with the properties of natural compounds.

Keep in mind that the majority of aromatherapists are self-employed. Math, business, and computer courses will help you develop the skills you need to be successful at running a business. Aromatherapists also need good communication and interpersonal skills to be sensitive to their clients. English, speech, and psychology classes can help you sharpen your ability to interact constructively with other people.

Eva-Marie Lind is an aromatherapist, author, and former dean of the Aromatherapy Department of the Australasian College of Herbal Studies in Lake Oswego, Oregon. She has worked in the field of aromatherapy for over 15 years. According to Lind, "Education is the key to good aromatherapy. There is so much to learn, and it takes real dedication to study."

Postsecondary Training

In 1999, the National Association for Holistic Aromatherapy (NAHA) established criteria for aromatherapy education that have been voluntarily adopted by a number of schools and education programs. NAHA guidelines recommend that aromatherapy education include courses on topics such as the history of aromatherapy, physiology, production of essential oils, botany, chemistry, safety and methods of application, and business planning.

While the NAHA provides a listing of schools complying with its guidelines, there are also other schools, seminars, and distance learning courses that offer training in aromatherapy. Be aware, however, that the quality of programs can vary. Take the time to call the schools or organizations that interest you. Ask how their programs are set up. For correspondence courses (or distance courses), ask if you will be able to talk to a teacher. How will you be evaluated? Are there tests? How are the tests taken and graded? Try to talk with current students. Ask how they are treated and what they learn. Ask what you receive when you graduate from the program. Will you receive help with job placement? Access to insurance programs? Other benefits? Depending on the program you pick, the length of study ranges from short workshops to four-year college courses. Vocational schools, major universities, and naturopathic colleges are increasingly offering training in aromatherapy.

Most aromatherapists are also professionals in other fields. Consider whether you would want to combine aromatherapy with a "base" profession, such as chiropractic, massage therapy, nursing, or some other field. These base fields require additional education and certification as well as licensing. If you decide to add aromatherapy to another profession, learn the requirements for certification or licensing that apply to that profession. Adding aromatherapy to another profession requires a comprehensive understanding of both fields.

Certification or Licensing

The National Association for Holistic Aromatherapy offers voluntary registration to aromatherapists who meet minimum educational standards from an association-approved academic institution and pass an examination, which focuses on four knowledge areas basic concepts of aromatherapy, scientific principles, administration, and professional issues. Registration must be renewed every five years. Contact the association for more information on registration requirements.

If you choose to combine aromatherapy with another profession, you must meet the national and local requirements for that field in addition to aromatherapy requirements.

Other Requirements
According to Eva-Marie Lind, "Aromatherapy demands love and passion at its roots. You need to honor, respect, and celebrate the beauty of this field."

You must also enjoy disseminating knowledge because clients often have many questions. More practically, it takes a good nose and a certain sensitivity to successfully treat clients through aromatherapy. It takes good listening skills and immense creativity to understand each client's personal issues and decide on the best means of administering a treatment. Which essential oils or combination of oils should you choose? Should you use a bath, a compress, a massage, or inhalation? What parts of the body are the best avenues for delivering the remedy?

Aromatherapists must be good self-teachers who are interested in continuing education. This is a relatively new field that is developing and changing rapidly. To stay competitive and successful, you need to keep up with the changing trends, products, and technologies that affect the field. Like most healing professions, aromatherapy is a lifelong education process for the practitioner.

EXPLORING

There are many ways to explore the field of aromatherapy to see if it is for you. For one, there are many books and specialized periodicals available on the subject. Get a glimpse of the types of knowledge you need for the field. Find out whether it is too scientific or not scientific enough. Look in your local library for books and magazines that show you what a typical student of aromatherapy might be learning.

Visit health food stores. The staff members of health food stores are often very helpful. Most have books, magazines, and newspapers about many kinds of alternative health care, including aromatherapy. Ask about essential oils, and ask for the names of aromatherapists in the area. Find out if there are garden clubs that you can join—particularly ones that specialize in herbs. Consider taking up cooking. This could give you practice in selecting herbs and seasonings and blending them to create different aromas and flavors.

Contact local and national professional organizations. Some offer student memberships or free seminars. Check out their Web sites. They have a lot of valuable information and good links to other alternative health care sites. Join online forums and discussion groups where you can communicate with professionals from all over the country and the world. Some distance learning courses are open to students of all ages. Check into them.

If you find you have a real interest in aromatherapy, another way to explore the field is to seek a mentor, a professional in the field who is willing to help you learn. Tell everyone you know that you are interested in aromatherapy. Someone is bound to have a connection with someone you could call for an informational interview. Perhaps you could spend a day "shadowing" an aromatherapist to see what the work is like. If you are unable to find an aromatherapy specialist, you could call spas and salons in search of professionals who use aromatherapy in their work. Perhaps some would be willing to speak to you about their day-to-day work. Make an appointment and experience an aromatherapy treatment. Taking it a step further, you could explore the possibility of getting a part-time job at an establishment that employs aromatherapists.

EMPLOYERS

Most aromatherapists are self-employed. They run their own small businesses and build their own clientele. Some set up their own offices, but many build their businesses by working in the offices of other professionals and giving aromatherapy treatments as supplements to the treatments provided by the resident professionals. Many different kinds of employers are looking for skilled aromatherapists. In the cosmetic industry, beauticians, cosmeticians, and massage therapists employ aromatherapists to give treatments that complement their own. Spas, athletic clubs, resorts, and cruise ships may hire aromatherapists on a full-time basis. These types of employment may be temporary or seasonal.

In the health care industry, chiropractors, acupuncturists, and other alternative therapy practitioners and clinics may offer aromatherapy in addition to their basic services. Hospitals, nursing homes, hospice centers, and other medical establishments are beginning to recognize the physiological and psychological benefits of aromatherapy for their patients.

STARTING OUT

Because the practice of aromatherapy may be incorporated into numerous other professions, there are many ways to enter the field. How you enter depends on how you want to use aromatherapy. Is your interest in massage therapy, skin care, or hair care? Do you want to be a nurse, doctor, acupuncturist, or chiropractor? Are you interested in becoming an instructor or writer? Once you are certified in another area, you need to search for clinics, salons, spas, and other establishments that are looking for professionals who use aromatherapy in their treatments. School career services offices are also a way to find work. Classified ads in newspapers and trade magazines list positions in the related fields.

Networking can be an important source of job opportunities. Networking is simply getting to know others and exchanging ideas with them. Go to association meetings and conventions. Talk to people in the field. Job openings are often posted at such gatherings.

ADVANCEMENT

Aromatherapists can advance to many different levels, depending on their goals, ambitions, aspirations, and willingness to work. Those who are self-employed can increase their clientele and open their own offices or even a salon. Those who are employed at a spa or salon could become a department director or the director of the entire spa or salon. They might start a private practice or open a spa or salon.

As their skills and knowledge grow, aromatherapists may be sought after to teach and train other aromatherapists in seminars or at schools that offer aromatherapy programs or courses. Others become consultants or write books and articles. A few start their own aromatherapy product lines of esthetic or therapeutic products. Some may become involved in growing the plants that are the sources of essential oils. Still others work in distilling, analyzing, or blending the oils.

This new field is growing so rapidly that the potential for advancement is enormous. The field has so many facets that the directions for growth are as great as your imagination and determination. A public relations representative from the National Association for Holistic Aromatherapists says, "If you are self-motivated, creative, and have a talent for any aspect of aromatherapy, the sky is the limit. It is what you make it."

EARNINGS

Since aromatherapists work in such a variety of settings, and aromatherapy is often a supplementary therapy added to other professional training, it is particularly difficult to make statements about average earnings in the field. Government agencies do not yet have wage statistics for the field. The national professional associations have not yet developed surveys of their members that give reliable information.

For those who are self-employed in any profession, earnings depend on the amount of time they work and the amount they charge per hour. Experienced professional aromatherapists estimate that hourly rates can range from $25 to $65 for beginning aromatherapists and instructors. Rates increase with experience to between $75 and $100 per hour. Based on those rates, a beginning aromatherapist who charges $25 an hour and averages 10 appointments per week will earn around $13,000. According to the U.S. Department of Labor, in 2005 the median annual salary for people engaged in personal care and service occupations (the category aromatherapy would fall into) earned a median salary of $18,490, with the bottom 10 percent earning $12,920 per year and the top 10 percent $35,580 or more. Established aromatherapists who have a solid client base report earning $25,000 to $45,000.

The hourly rate an aromatherapist charges depends on his or her level of expertise, the type of clientele served, and even the area of the country. In many of the larger cities and much of the West Coast, people are already more aware and accepting of alternative health therapies. In those areas, higher hourly rates will be more accepted. Where such therapies are practically unknown, lower rates will apply. Another consideration for the self-employed is that they must provide their own insurance and retirement plans and pay for their supplies and other business expenses.

An aromatherapist with determination, creativity, and initiative can find jobs that pay well. Some who run exclusive spas or develop their own lines of aromatherapy products are reported to earn $70,000 to $80,000 or more, annually.

Aromatherapists who are primarily employed in other professions, such as massage therapists, chiropractors, cosmetologists, and nurses, can expect to make the salaries that are average for their profession. Those professionals who use aromatherapy as a supportive therapy to their primary profession tend to have higher incomes than those who specialize in aromatherapy. The addition of aromatherapy to their profession will probably enhance their clients' and their own satisfaction, but it may not increase their income.

WORK ENVIRONMENT

Aromatherapists work in a service-oriented environment, in which the main duty involves understanding and helping their clients. The surroundings are usually clean, peaceful, and pleasant. They work with very potent substances (strong essential oils), but most aromatherapists love the scents and the experience of the oils. They often spend a great deal of time on their feet. They sometimes work long or inconsistent hours, such as weekends and evenings, to accommodate their clients' needs.

Aromatherapists are people-oriented. Those who are self-employed must be highly motivated and able to work alone. Aromatherapists who work in clinics, spas, hospitals, resorts, and other locations need to be able to work well with others.

OUTLOOK

Aromatherapy has been growing very rapidly and is gathering steam in the United States. Opportunities are increasing rapidly as public awareness of alternative therapies is increasing.

The status of aromatherapy in European and other countries may provide a glimpse of the future of the field in the United States. In Great Britain and France, for example, more doctors have embraced aromatherapy, and these services are covered by major health plans. If the United States follows this lead, new doors will open in this field. In general, the outlook is very good for aromatherapy because of an overwhelming increase in public awareness and interest.

FOR MORE INFORMATION

For information regarding state regulations for massage therapists and general information on therapeutic massage, contact
American Massage Therapy Association
500 Davis Street, Suite 900
Evanston, IL 60201-4695
Tel: 877-905-2700
Email: info@amtamassage.org
http://www.amtamassage.org

For information on registration, contact
Aromatherapy Registration Council
5940 SW Hood Avenue
Portland, OR 97039-3719
Tel: 503-244-0726
Email: info@aromatherapycouncil.org
http://www.aromatherapycouncil.org

The National Association for Holistic Aromatherapy has developed guidelines for aromatherapy training. See its Web site for a listing of schools in compliance with these guidelines.

National Association for Holistic Aromatherapy
3327 West Indian Trail Road, PMB 144
Spokane, WA 99208-4762
Tel: 509-325-3419
Email: info@naha.org
http://www.naha.org

For general information about aromatherapy and education options, visit the following Web site:

AromaWeb
http://www.aromaweb.com

Barbers

OVERVIEW

Barbers shampoo, cut, trim, and style hair and shave, trim, and shape beards. While barbers are formally trained to perform other services such as coloring and perming hair, most barbers in barbershops do not offer these services. Barbers may also call themselves *barber-stylists,* and a few may even refer to themselves as *tonsorial artists,* an old-fashioned term which is derived from a Latin word meaning "to shear." Approximately 13,600 barbers are employed in the United States.

HISTORY

Barbering boasts a long and rich history. The word barber is derived from the Latin word *barba,* meaning beard. Archaeologists tell us that the cave dwellers of 20,000 years ago tweezed their whiskers with clam shells. There are several Biblical references that reflect the Egyptian preoccupation with facial hair and shaving. As early as 500 B.C., barbers began establishing themselves in Greece, and their sidewalk shops became gathering places for discussions of sports, philosophy, politics, and gossip. Of course, not everyone appreciated the talkative barber: When King Archelaus, who ruled Macedon from 413 to 399 B.C., was asked by his barber how he wanted his hair cut, he replied, "In silence." Greek barbers also served as dieticians, as well as setting broken bones, giving enemas, bloodletting, and performing minor surgeries.

During the Dark Ages, barbers began to be known as barber-surgeons. They performed medical procedures such as bloodletting, tooth extraction, and minor surgeries. In England, during the reign of Henry VIII, from 1509 to 1547, the two professions

QUICK FACTS.

School Subjects
Business
Health

Personal Skills
Artistic
Mechanical/manipulative

Work Environment
Primarily indoors
Primarily one location

Minimum Education Level
Some postsecondary training

Salary Range
$14,770 to $21,760 to
$36,180+

Certification or Licensing
Required by all states

Outlook
More slowly than the average

DOT
330

GOE
11.04.01

NOC
6271

O*NET-SOC
39-5011.00

were separated by an act forbidding barber-surgeons to perform any surgical procedures except tooth extractions and bloodletting. In 1745, the final split between barbers and surgeons occurred under an act of George II. Following this act, the barber profession gradually declined to the status of wigmakers, as wigs became the rage during the 18th century. By the end of the 1700s, nearly all barbers, except those in remote areas, had ceased practicing surgical and dental procedures. Bloodletting was not abandoned as a practice until the 19th century, long after George Washington's personal physician had literally bled him to death while attempting to cure a windpipe infection.

The period between the Civil War and World War II was truly the heyday of the American barbershop. The familiar red and white pole—symbolizing the bandages used on a bleeding patient—was a welcoming sight to a weary traveler. In a short time, the dirty, scruffy, smelly stranger would be transformed into a bathed, shaved, perfumed, and shorn gentleman. His boots would be shined, his pants pressed, and he may even have been offered a cigar and a mug of beer. During his grooming session, he was sure to be informed of local employment opportunities and where he might find room and board. Many barbershops were open 12 hours a day and even early Sunday mornings, when, for a few nickels, a man could get his face lathered and shaved before church. As in ancient Greece and Rome, barbershops were places of gossip, socializing, and often live music (the famous "barbershop quartet" style of singing in four-part harmony).

Today, barbershops—which once outnumbered saloons in many towns—are dwindling as beauty salons and spas flourish. With the gender line steadily eroding in matters of cosmetology, many men are turning to full-service shops for manicures and special hairstyles and procedures. However, most barbers have a loyal clientele, which steadily increases the longer a barber is in business. According to an executive of a national association for barbers, the average barber today has been on the job for 27.1 years.

Fashion and imitation have always played a significant role in the evolution of hairstyles. In earlier times, much like today, styles that met with disapproval among one generation became the accepted styles for the next. Barbers have observed various trends in business based upon the styles of the celebrities of the day. For example, many barbers saw business slow down gradually following the advent of Beatlemania and longer hairstyles for men. In the 1980s, the movie *Top Gun* spurred a renewed popularity of the short haircut. Today, the hairstyles of pop stars and actors, as well as professional athletes, continue to have a strong influence on the hairstyles of the American public.

A barber uses electric clippers to cut the hair of a young boy.
(*PhotoDisc*)

THE JOB

Most barbers in barbershops focus primarily on the basics of men's
grooming needs: haircutting and trimming, shampooing, styling,
and beard and mustache trimming and shaping. Many include a
brief facial, scalp, and/or neck massage. While some barbers do
perform other services, such as tinting or bleaching, most find that
few of their customers seek such services, and those that do are more

likely to head for a full-service salon. Shaving is far less common in barbershops today than it once was. The safety razor has made shaving at home a relatively quick and easy task, and the art of the straight-edge shave is little more than a relic of tonsorial history.

Most customers who frequent barbershops are men, but some women—particularly those with short hair—do patronize barbers. Likewise, most barbers are men, but the field includes some female barbers as well.

The equipment barbers use—clippers, razors, shears, combs, brushes, and so forth—must be kept in antiseptic condition. Often barbers must supply their own equipment. Barbers who operate their own shops must handle the details of answering phones and setting appointments, ordering supplies and paying bills, maintaining equipment, and keeping records. If they employ other barbers, they are responsible for the hiring and performance of their staff as well. Barbershops range from one-person operations to larger shops with many chairs and operators.

REQUIREMENTS

High School

Many states require that barbers be high school graduates, although a few states require only an eighth-grade education. High school students considering a career as a barber might find it helpful to take courses in health and business. Involvement in theater can provide you with opportunities to practice working on hair and attempting to create different styles as well as give you the opportunity to develop the people skills you will need later when dealing with the public.

Postsecondary Training

Generally, a barber must complete a certain number of hours of barber school (ranging from 1,000 to 2,000 hours, depending on the state). Most states offer programs that include classroom work, demonstrations, and hands-on work and can be completed in 10 to 24 months. The barber must then pass an examination that includes a written test (and sometimes an oral test) and a practical examination to demonstrate mastery of skills. He or she must also obtain a health certificate. In selecting a barber school, a student should be sure the school meets (and preferably exceeds) the state's requirements for licensing. Some schools have waiting lists, so it may be prudent to apply early.

At one time, a one- to two-year apprenticeship was required in many states before a barber was "full-fledged"; this practice is

becoming less common as formal training is increasingly empha-
sized. In a few rural areas, an apprenticeship can take the place of
formal education, but this is an uncommon and difficult way to
acquire sufficient skill and knowledge.

Certification or Licensing

All barbers must be licensed to practice in the state in which they
work, although the requirements vary from state to state. Some
states have licensing reciprocity agreements that enable barbers to
practice in another state without being retested. Some states require
that barbers be at least 18 years old in order to be licensed.

Unions were once prevalent among barbers, but they are becoming less common, especially in rural areas. Today there are fewer
barbers in the workforce than there were decades ago, and a large
percentage (48 percent) are self-employed. The United Food and
Commercial Workers International Union is the principal union that
organizes barbers.

Other Requirements

Barbering requires good finger dexterity and stamina, since barbers
are required to be on their feet most of the day (although work
environments can often be adapted to accommodate workers with
disabilities or special needs). Barbers should themselves be neat and
well-groomed because they work in close proximity to their customers. Tact and patience are important characteristics, as is being
a good listener. The ability to easily carry on light conversation
also is important. Roy Bollhoffer, owner of Roy's Barbershop in
Highland Park, Illinois, stresses the importance of being a "people-
person." Says Bollhoffer about being a barber, "If you don't like
people, you're in trouble." Bollhoffer has owned his barbershop for
34 years; he bought it from a barber who started his business just
after World War I. Nearly all of Bollhoffer's customers have been
with him for many years, and quite a few have patronized his shop
for even longer than the 34 years Bollhoffer has been there. Like
many barbers, Bollhoffer finds that once customers find a barber
they like, they stick with him or her until the customers die or move,
or until the barber retires.

To be successful, barbers must understand the importance their
customers place on their appearances and seriously strive to provide
a look that pleases their customers. An executive in a national association for barbers notes, "You're in the business of making people
happy." Barbers should have a sense of form and style in order
to determine what looks would be most flattering for individual

customers. A barber must also recognize when a style desired by a customer isn't suited to the customer's features or hair type in order to avoid customer dissatisfaction. These situations require firmness and diplomacy.

EXPLORING

If you are interested in this career, try finding part-time employment in a barbershop or beauty salon to gain exposure to the nature of the work and the working conditions. Another avenue of exploration might be to call a barber school and ask for an opportunity to tour the facilities, observe classes, and question instructors. Of course, nothing compares to talking to someone with firsthand experience; a chat with a local barber is a sure and easy way to obtain helpful and informative feedback.

EMPLOYERS

There are approximately 13,600 barbers employed in the United States. A barber's domain is almost exclusively the barbershop. While some barbers may find work in a full-service styling salon, most of these businesses are seeking stylists with broader training and experience. Most barbers are self-employed, either owning their own shops or renting a chair at a barbershop. In the days before beauty salons were so prevalent—and before men frequented them—nearly all men had their hair cut by barbers. Today, these men still account for a significant portion of barbershops' clientele, so opportunities for barbers may be better in areas with a higher concentration of older men. Some barbers are employed as teachers or trainers at barber schools, and some may also serve as inspectors for the state boards of barber examiners.

STARTING OUT

In most states, the best way (and often the only way) to enter the field of barbering is to graduate from a barber school that meets the state's requirements for licensing and to pass the state's licensing examination. Nearly all barber schools assist graduates with the process of finding employment opportunities. As barbershops are few in many areas, calling or visiting a barbershop is an excellent way to find employment. In some areas, there may be barbering unions which may be helpful in one's job search. While a part-time job in a barbershop or beauty shop can be helpful in determining one's level of interest in the field, satisfying the graduation requirements of an accredited barber school and becoming licensed is usually the only way to enter this occupation.

ADVANCEMENT

The most common form of advancement in the barbering profession is owning one's own shop. This requires business experience and skill as well as proficiency in the barbering profession; and of course start-up requires capital outlay. Those who are successful as owners do reap higher earnings than barbers who rent a booth in a shop or are paid on a commission basis. Some even go on to own a chain of barbershops. In larger barbershops, there may be opportunities for management, but these are relatively rare. The longer a barber is on the job, though, the larger the clientele (and thus the security and income) becomes.

Barbers can increase their opportunities for advancement by becoming licensed as cosmetologists and working in larger beauty shops that provide more complicated, varied, and advanced services. Opportunities for management or specializing in certain services are increasingly plentiful in full-service salons. Many states require a separate license for cosmetology, but often barbering training can be applied toward a cosmetology license. In a few states, the two licenses are combined into one hairstyling license.

Related career opportunities may exist if a barber wishes to become an instructor at a barber school or an inspector for a state board of barber examiners.

EARNINGS

Incomes can vary widely depending on a barber's experience, the location of the shop, the number of hours worked, tipping habits of the clientele, and whether or not a barber owns the business. The personality and initiative of a barber also impacts the ability to draw a loyal following. The U.S. Department of Labor reports that the median annual income for full-time, salaried barbers, including tips, was $21,760 in 2005. The highest paid 10 percent earned more than $36,180 per year, while the lowest paid 10 percent earned less than $14,770 annually. Many established barbers and barber/owners earn incomes that well exceed the median.

One of the most frequently cited downsides to being a barber is a lack of benefits, particularly where there are no unions. Many barbers cannot get group insurance, and the cost of individual policies can be high. Also, since most barbers are either self-employed or working for small shops, benefits such as retirement plans, paid vacations, sick days, and so forth are often the exception to the rule.

WORK ENVIRONMENT

Barbers generally enjoy pleasant work surroundings. The barber-shop environment is usually friendly, clean, and comfortable. Many barbers can set their own hours, and although many work Saturdays, they typically take Sundays and weeknights off. Of course, this depends largely on the schedules of their clientele; barbers whose clientele consists mostly of retirees rarely find the need to work evenings. Stress levels and job pressures are lower than is the case with most jobs. Established barbers enjoy a unique security in that their clients are usually very loyal and always need haircuts. Most barbers don't share the fears of layoffs and other job insecurities common to other professions. Compared to their cosmetologist counterparts, barbers are exposed to fewer hair and nail chemicals, which also enhances the work environment. Most barbers have been on the job for many years, and there is clearly a great deal of pride and job enjoyment among barbers. This is a good profession for those who enjoy the company of other people.

OUTLOOK

As the cosmetology industry has flourished, the number of old-fashioned barbershops has waned. More and more, men have turned to styling salons rather than barbershops to have their styling and grooming needs met. In addition, only a small number of cosmetology school graduates are getting barbering licenses. The U.S. Department of Labor predicts that employment for barbers will grow more slowly than the average for all occupations through 2014.

Many job openings will result from the need to replace retired workers. And since there are few qualified candidates, those entering the field may find good opportunities, depending on their location. Says Roy Bollhoffer, "I had another barber here with me for 27 years, but he retired. I'd love to find another barber to bring in, but there is a serious shortage of barbers now. And there will always be people who want to go to a barber. I've made a very nice living here." In all likelihood, the outlook for this profession will be different for various cities, states, and regions of the country.

FOR MORE INFORMATION

For information about the profession as well as a list of licensed training schools, contact

National Accrediting Commission of Cosmetology Arts and
  Sciences
4401 Ford Avenue, Suite 1300
Alexandria, VA 22302-1432
Tel: 703-600-7600
http://www.naccas.org

Color Analysts and Image Consultants

OVERVIEW

Color analysts assess their clients' coloring, including skin tone and hair and eye color, and teach them how to use their most flattering colors in clothing and makeup. *Image consultants* usually work with people in business, helping them present themselves in a professional manner.

Color and image consultants offer programs for individual women or men, for professional or social organizations, or for all the employees of one company. Some work with retailers, teaching salespersons about color and style and presenting in-store workshops.

HISTORY

In their book, *Color Me Beautiful's Looking Your Best,* Mary Spillane and Christine Sherlock cite a study by Albert Mehrabian. He found that the impression we make on others is made up of 55 percent appearance and behavior, 38 percent speech, and only 7 percent the content of what we say. These figures clearly show the importance of presenting yourself well in business, social, and other settings. Beauty consultants have been around for some time, but their work is constantly evolving. Because our society is increasingly mobile, and we change jobs more often than our parents did, we are constantly establishing ourselves with new groups. In addition, television has increased our awareness of appearance and what it tells us about the individual. Projecting a positive image through our appearance and behavior helps us gain acceptance

School Subjects
Art
Business
Theater/dance

Personal Skills
Artistic
Communication/ideas

Work Environment
Primarily indoors
Primarily multiple locations

Minimum Education Level
Some postsecondary training

Salary Range
$13,400 to $20,610 to
$100,000+

Certification or Licensing
Recommended

Outlook
About as fast as the average

DOT
N/A

GOE
N/A

NOC
6481

O*NET-SOC
N/A

from social and business contacts, fit into the workplace, and meet the public.

In 1980, with the publication of Carole Jackson's book, *Color Me Beautiful,* many people, especially women, began to think about what they purchased and wore in a different way. No longer willing to accept whatever fashion decreed, they wanted colors and styles that enhanced their individual appearance. By the time more than 20 million people had read this *New York Times* bestseller, clothing manufacturers, cosmetic companies, and retailers felt the impact of the new consumer demand.

In the meantime, other businesses were dealing with their increased need for employees with technological backgrounds. Such employees often were totally involved in the technical aspects of their work and unconcerned about the impression they made on coworkers, clients, and the general public. Many companies began to provide training to help employees project better images, increasing the demand for image consultants.

THE JOB

Most color and image consultants are entrepreneurs, meaning that they own and manage their businesses and assume all the risks. They may work with individuals, groups, or both. Christine Sherlock, director of training and communications for Color Me Beautiful, reports that her firm trains color analysts in color and its use in wardrobe and makeup. Those who wish to become image consultants take additional training so they can help clients work on their overall appearance and grooming, as well as improve their voices, body language, and etiquette. Consultants also may learn to coach clients on dealing with the public and the media.

Susan Fignar, president of S. Fignar & Associates Inc., is a corporate image trainer and consultant who has been quoted in *Cosmopolitan,* the *Wall Street Journal,* and the *Chicago Tribune.* She works with some of the country's largest corporations and offers a variety of corporate programs and interactive workshops. Fignar says she provides training that helps people bring out their best personal and professional presence. Like other entrepreneurs, her business requires constant sales and marketing to obtain clients.

Her training sessions deal with such topics as making a good first impression, everyday etiquette, developing self-esteem and confidence, verbal communication, body language and facial expression, overall appearance, and appropriate dress for every occasion. She notices an increasing demand for her services in dress code consulting and training sessions on business casual dress.

Sherlock says consultants get satisfaction from helping others look better and feel good about themselves. "When a consultant helps a client with her wardrobe," she says, "the client not only saves money; she uses 100 percent of her wardrobe and no longer complains she has nothing to wear."

REQUIREMENTS

High School

If you are interested in this work, you will benefit from taking classes and being involved in activities that develop your ability to communicate and increase your understanding of visual effects. Helpful classes to take include English, speech, and drama. Activities to consider participating in include drama clubs and debate teams. In drama club you may have the opportunity to help apply makeup, select wardrobes, and learn about the emotional impact appearances can have. Art classes are also helpful; especially classes that teach color theory. Since many people in this line of work are entrepreneurs, consider taking any business, bookkeeping, or accounting classes that will give you the skills to run your own business.

Any part-time job working with the public is valuable. You can gain excellent experience from selling clothing or cosmetics in department stores, from working in beauty salons or spas, or from working as waitpersons. Volunteer work that involves working with people will also help you hone your people skills.

Postsecondary Training

There are no formal, standardized training programs for color analysts and image consultants. In general, Susan Fignar recommends attending seminars or classes on color, psychology, training methods, and communications. She adds that a degree in liberal arts, with a major in education, is a plus for those working at the corporate level.

Color Me Beautiful has trainers who travel throughout the country. They offer people who wish to become consultants basic classes in skin care, makeup, and color analysis and advanced classes in such subjects as theory of style and presentation. Most classes take one or two days for a single topic; most working consultants take at least one new class each year.

If you get to know a color analyst or image consultant personally, you may be able to arrange an informal internship of your own. Some people begin their careers in this field by working as apprentices to other consultants. Color Me Beautiful accepts a two-month apprenticeship with an approved consultant.

Certification or Licensing

The Association of Image Consultants International (AICI) provides three levels of certification: first level certification, certified image professional, and certified image master. Contact the AICI for more information.

Other Requirements

Christine Sherlock recommends this field for those who like to work with and help other people and says an interest in fashion and style are also obviously very helpful. A general flair for art and design would prove useful. Analysts and consultants should be friendly, outgoing, supportive of others, able to offer constructive feedback, and open to change. There are few disabilities that would prevent an individual from doing this work.

Susan Fignar believes experience in the business world, especially in management and public contact, is essential for corporate consulting. She says that corporate consultants must be mature, poised, and professional to have credibility, and that people are usually between the ages of 33 and 40 when they enter this field.

EXPLORING

One way to explore this career is to arrange for a personal visit to a consultant. The AICI, for example, offers lists of qualified consultants throughout the country (see the end of this article for contact information).

There are several books you can read to learn more about color and image consulting. Christine Sherlock recommends *Color Me Beautiful* by Carole Jackson (Ballantine Books, 1987), *Color Me Beautiful's Looking Your Best: Color, Makeup, and Style* by Mary Spillane and Christine Sherlock (Madison Books, 2002), and *Women of Color* by Darlene Mathis (SPCK and Triangle, 1999). Susan Fignar recommends *Image Consulting: The New Career* by Joan Timberlake (Acropolis Books, 1983), which discusses the various areas in which image consultants specialize. Because networking is so important in getting clients, she also suggests *Networlding: Building Relationships and Opportunities for Success* by Melissa Giovagnoli (Jossey-Bass, 2000). Local libraries should have additional books on color, fabrics, style, etiquette, and body language.

EMPLOYERS

For the most part, color analysts and image consultants are self-employed. They run their own consulting businesses, which allows them the freedom to decide what image consulting services they wish to offer. For example, some consultants concentrate on working with corporate clients; other consultants may also advise individuals. Consultants may get the products they sell from one company, such as Color Me Beautiful, or they may offer a range of products and services that provide ways for clients to feel good about themselves. Those in apprenticeships and consultants just entering the field may work for consultants who have already established their businesses.

STARTING OUT

Some consultants enter the field through apprenticeships. Susan Fignar began by working in advertising, where she had extensive experience in meeting planning and often was responsible for company visitors. She eventually attended a training program on fashion and image consulting. She says there are many routes to entering this field.

ADVANCEMENT

Workers can advance from color analyst to image consultant to trainer by gaining experience and additional education. Christine Sherlock began as an apprentice and has advanced through various positions with Color Me Beautiful. Salon and department store employees would advance along the path their employers have laid out.

Susan Fignar hopes to expand her business by adding new clients, taking advantage of new trends, developing training for future image consultants, and forming alliances with consultants who offer related services. This is par for the course for all self-employed analysts and consultants. She has had her own business for seven years and says it takes three to five years to get a corporate consulting business established.

EARNINGS

A color analyst's or image consultant's earnings are determined by the number of hours the consultant works, the type of clientele, and the consultant's location. Christine Sherlock says earnings are highest in New York City and Southern California. Some consultants increase their incomes by offering additional services. Susan Fignar estimates that earnings start at under $20,000 but can reach $75,000 or more for top performers. Since many color analysts and image consultants own their own businesses, it may also be helpful to consider that some small-business owners may earn only about $15,000 a year, while the most successful may make $100,000 or more. The U.S. Department of Labor reports that median annual earnings for hairstylists and cosmetologists were $20,610 in 2005, with 10 percent making $13,400 or less and 10 percent making $37,380 or more.

Christine Sherlock points out such advantages as owning your own business, flexible hours, controlling your own time, and opportunity for personal growth and development. Because most consultants are self-employed, they must provide their own insurance and other benefits.

WORK ENVIRONMENT

Many consultants work from their homes. Color consultants also work in salons, boutiques, day spas, and retail areas. The work is indoors and may involve travel. Christine Sherlock comments that the work has changed her life and that she loves everything she has done in the field.

Susan Fignar works at corporate sites and training facilities, speaks before various organizations, and has appeared on radio and television. She has contact with management and with human resources and training departments. Her work schedule has busy and slow periods, but she usually works from 40 to 50 hours a week and sometimes makes evening presentations. She describes her work as exciting, draining, and full of time constraints.

OUTLOOK

The employment of personal appearance workers is expected to grow as fast as the average through 2014, according to the *Occupational Outlook Handbook,* mainly due to increasing population, incomes, and demand for cosmetology services.

Christine Sherlock says the economy has little effect on color consulting. During sluggish times, people still want the lift that such beauty services give them. The demand for consultants is growing steadily, and she believes self-employed people with successful businesses aren't likely to be out of work. The field is evolving, with new opportunities in corporate work.

Susan Fignar says corporate consultants are affected by downsizing because when companies cut personnel they also reduce training. "Right now," she says, "the field is growing." She says the hot topics are casual dress for business, etiquette, communications, and public image. Fignar feels security comes from constantly working to build your consulting business. She advises consultants to develop a 60-

second sales pitch so they're always ready to describe their services to any prospective client they meet.

FOR MORE INFORMATION

This organization has information on continuing education, mentorship programs, and certification.
Association of Image Consultants International
100 East Grand Avenue, Suite 330
Des Moines, IA 50309-1835
Tel: 515-282-5500
Email: info@aici.org
http://www.aici.org

This company provides information on contacting local consultants. Check out its Web site for information on their products.
Color Me Beautiful
http://www.colormebeautiful.com

──────── INTERVIEW ────────

Dr. Joyce Knudsen has been an image consultant for more than 30 years and is the owner of The ImageMaker Inc. (To learn more about her career and services, visit http://www.imagemaker1.com.) She discussed her career with the editors of Careers in Focus: Cosmetology.

Q. Tell us about your business.

A. The ImageMaker Inc. is an image resource company that trains people worldwide on all facets of image, including personality, behavior, self-esteem coaching, and personal development.

Q. What type of educational path did you pursue to become an image consultant?

A. I advocate higher education, so I received a B.A. in communications, an M.S.A. in business administration, and a Ph.D. in human services with emphasis on self-image.

Q. Take us through a day in your life as an image consultant. What are your typical tasks/responsibilities?

A. My days are atypical of image consultants who do color, makeup, etc. My day begins with answering e-mails, returning calls from the day before, writing proposals, helping students with their assignments [Knudsen also works as a professor at a local college], and writing. My tasks are being there for all of my clients.

Q. How important is certification to career development and advancement?

A. Highly. I have more than 12 certifications and was the first person in the industry to earn the Association of Image Consultants International–Certified Image Master designation. It is my belief that certification is crucial to understanding the concepts of any field. I have over eight certifications in behavior/personality alone!

Q. What do you like most and least about your job?

A. I love to help people and see them realize their dreams. I don't think most people understand the time, effort, and love that goes into what I give to my clients. The value is sometimes unappreciated.

Q. What advice would you give to high school students who are interested in this career?

A. One must have communication skills, have knowledge of operating a business, and understand people. Students would benefit from working in retail stores, taking speech and communication classes, and attending image seminars.

Cosmeticians

OVERVIEW

Cosmeticians, also referred to as *estheticians* and *skin care specialists*, specialize in skin care, providing an array of services from applying facial masks, peels, and herbal wraps, to massages, skin analysis, exfoliation, deep cleansing, product recommendations, and makeup application. In addition, cosmeticians provide hair removal services. Most cosmeticians work in beauty salons, day spas, and hotel resorts. Some work with dermatologists and cosmetic surgeons to prepare patients before surgery and during their recovery. There are approximately 30,000 skin care specialists employed in the United States.

HISTORY

The role of the cosmetician today originates from a long history of pampering and leisurely self-care, which began centuries ago in the public baths and spas of Asia and Europe. Ancient Babylonians, Egyptians, and Romans renewed and invigorated themselves in public baths. Archeological evidence suggests that in ancient Egypt cosmetics were also used to enhance the appearance of the skin. Products included ingredients such as special soils, wax, honey, and oils that were formulated into masks, makeup, and lipsticks. In ancient Greece, Hippocrates, known as the father of medicine, contributed to the development of *esthetics* (scientific skin care). Archeological remains suggest that Greek women used mixtures of plant roots and yeast to try to eliminate freckles and applied masks made with bread crumbs and milk to prevent wrinkles. Artifacts from ancient Roman society include recipes for creams made from fruit juices, honey, and olive oil. Soothing therapies, still practiced today, from Shiatsu massage to potent herbal treatments, have been passed down from thousand-year-old traditions of the East.

During the Middle Ages interest in skin care and public baths waned in the Western world. Certain orders of nuns, however, devoted themselves to producing beauty products to support their convents. Perfume oils began to be used and the fragrance market was launched. The Renaissance saw skin care and cosmetics again become popular in large European cities. The manufacture of perfumes became a major industry. From writings of the 16th century, we find that many formulas and mixtures are very similar to modern cosmetic products. By the 17th and 18th centuries spas had gained the support of the medical establishment and once again became popular places. And by the 1800s, Europe's wealthy classes were spending months at a time relaxing and rejuvenating themselves at spas. It was not until the 1920s that spas caught on in the United States, and even then they were considered a luxury that only the very wealthy could afford.

Today, due to heightened health awareness, the need for more specialized beauty services, and increasing affordability of spa and salon services in the United States, cosmeticians are more in demand than ever before. Now more than just pamperers, cosmeticians are professionals and consultants, equipped with an awareness of skin conditions and allergies, as well as the scientific knowledge necessary to make recommendations based on biological and chemical analysis. As technical advancements in such areas as chemical peels and wrinkle reduction continue to boom, cosmeticians will become more prevalent and their services will be in greater demand.

THE JOB

The word *esthetic* comes from the Greek word meaning harmony, beauty, and perfection. Esthetics is based on an understanding of the skin's anatomy and function. Cosmeticians, or estheticians, work to improve the skin's condition and restore its functions. This discipline requires the cosmetician to get to know the client's skin and lifestyle and tailor treatments specifically for the client's needs. Cosmeticians offer a number of appearance-enhancing services that deal with the effects of pollution, lack of exercise, poor nutrition, and stress on the skin. The cosmetician's job may involve facials, massages, wraps and packs, hydrotherapy treatments, scalp treatments, hair removal services, color analysis, makeup services, and product sales. Before beginning to work with a client, the cosmetician will most likely consult with the individual to determine his or her goals and concerns. It is important that cosmeticians are clear with their clients as to what they should expect from their treatments.

For example, after the initial consultation for a facial, the cosmetician will need to perform a skin analysis in order to assess the client's water and oil levels and skin conditions—whether there are blackheads, lines, wrinkles, and so on. Once this information is determined, pre-cleansing, deep cleansing, exfoliation (the removal of dead skin), and extractions may follow, depending on the client's skin type. Cosmeticians often blend special cleansers and moisturizers themselves, according their clients' individual skin types.

The application of an appropriate mask for the patron's skin type may follow the cleansing and exfoliation process, along with neck, facial, and shoulder massages. Foot and hand massages may be included as well. In most states, cosmeticians are only licensed to perform hand, foot, and facial massages, and training for these services is usually provided in cosmetology programs. Full body massages require both further training and a special license.

While performing such procedures as extractions, which involve the removal of blackheads, whiteheads, and other skin debris, cosmeticians must be careful to protect themselves by using gloves and proper sanitation. These procedures are covered in cosmetician training programs and are regulated by law in most states.

Other services cosmeticians offer include wraps, packs, and hydrotherapy treatments. Often made of herbs, mud, or algae, these treatments remove or redistribute fat cells and retained body water in order to create a temporarily slimmer look. Some wraps and packs actually remove impurities from the body. Hydrotherapy treatments cleanse the body using seawater, fresh water, hot tubs, whirlpool baths, and hydrotherapy tubs.

Cosmeticians also provide cosmetics and makeup consultation and application services. They may assist clients in deciding what colors and makeup to use and how they should apply it to achieve the best results, whether it's for accentuating their features or covering blemishes.

Hair removal services, usually waxing and tweezing, are also offered. Electrolysis is another popular form of hair removal; however, since a special license is required to perform electrolysis, cosmeticians generally wax and tweeze unwanted hair from the face, eyebrows, and other parts of the body.

In addition to working with clients, cosmeticians are expected to keep their work areas clean and implements sanitized. In smaller salons, many make appointments and assist with day-to-day business activities. In larger salons, cosmeticians must be aware of keeping to appointment schedules. They may be juggling two or more clients, at different stages of treatment, at the same time.

Salon managers or *owners* have managerial responsibilities—accounting and record keeping, hiring, firing, and motivating workers, advertising and public relations, and ordering and stocking supplies and products.

People skills are very important for a cosmetician to have. A critical part of cosmeticians' jobs is to cultivate and maintain a growing clientele for themselves and their salons or spas. Cosmeticians should be sensitive to the client's comfort and have dexterity and a sense of artistry. If the cosmetician's style of skin care is not suited to the client, he or she should be willing to refer the client to another specialist. This builds goodwill toward the cosmetician and the salon or spa.

REQUIREMENTS

High School

If working as a cosmetician interests you, there are a number of classes you can take in high school to prepare for this job. Some vocational high schools offer classes that will prepare you specifically for cosmetology careers. If you are not attending a vocational high school, you should take science classes, such as biology, chemistry, and human anatomy. These classes will give you an understanding of how the body works as well as how chemicals react with each other. Scientific knowledge will come in handy when you consult with your clients about their allergies and skin conditions. In addition, science classes will give you the background necessary for understanding bacteriology and equipment sanitization—subjects you will most likely study in cosmetician courses following high school. Since you will be working with many different clients in this career, consider taking psychology courses, which will give you an understanding of people and their motivations. Take English and speech classes to develop your communication skills. Finally, take art courses. Art courses will allow you to work with your hands and help you develop your sense of color.

Postsecondary Training

Once you have completed high school, plan on enrolling in an accredited cosmetology school. A school's accreditation by the National Accrediting Commission of Cosmetology Arts and Sciences means that the school is meeting educational standards set by this national organization. It is important to make sure you will be going to a good school, because having a solid education from a respected program is one of your strongest assets when entering this field. You should also be aware of the licensing requirements for the state in which you hope to work. Make sure that the school you are interested in will allow you to meet these requirements. Depending on the school you choose to attend, you may enter a full cosmetology program to later specialize as a cosmetician, or you may enroll in a cosmetician or esthetician program. In either case your education should include study in skin care, massage techniques, specific areas of the law pertaining to the field, sanitation methods, makeup, and salon management.

Certification or Licensing

A cosmetician needs a license in most states, though the process, laws, and requirements vary from state to state. Licensing usually involves a test of one's skill and knowledge. A few states have reciprocity agreements, which would allow licensed cosmeticians to practice in a different state without additional formal training.

Other Requirements

A friendly, people-oriented personality and good listening skills are essential for this business. Because cosmeticians must work very closely with their clients, interpersonal skills are important. Sensitivity, tactfulness, and patience are particularly vital, especially when dealing with clients who may be unhappy about their appearance or with clients who have unreasonable expectations.

Flexibility is also a necessary trait, considering the long and irregular hours a full-time cosmetician works. Furthermore, the ability to sell has also become a desirable characteristic in cosmeticians, because retail sales are becoming a large part of salon offerings. Finally, a cosmetician should enjoy learning, as he or she may need to take continuing education workshops or seminars in order to keep up with licensing requirements and new developments in the field.

EXPLORING

One of the first activities you may consider in exploring this career is to get a facial or other service provided by a cosmetician. As a client, you will be able to observe the work setting and actually experience the procedure. Often people are best at providing services when they enjoy receiving the service or believe in its benefits.

Next, you may want to research this field by looking at association and trade magazines—the publications cosmeticians read to stay current with their field's trends. Trade publications such as *Skin Inc.* magazine (http://www.skininc.com/articles) will give you an idea of what current technical, legal, and fashion issues cosmeticians face.

You may choose to contact cosmetology schools to find out about cosmetician or esthetician programs in your area. Request informational brochures or course listings from the schools and speak to school advisers about the training involved and the nature of the work. A good way to locate cosmetology schools is to conduct an Internet search.

Also, once you have found a cosmetology school you are interested in, ask to set up an informational interview with an instructor or recent graduate. Go to the interview prepared to ask questions. What is the training like? What does this person enjoy about the job? What is the most difficult aspect of the work? By asking such questions you may be able to determine if the field is right for you.

You may also be able to set up an informational interview with a cosmetician who works at a spa or salon near you. Again, go to the interview prepared with questions. By networking in this fashion, you may also develop a mentor relationship. Then you may be able to spend time with your mentor at his or her place of work and observe everyday activities.

Getting a part-time position at a salon or spa on weekends or after school is an excellent way of exploring the field. Because you are working at the spa or salon on a regular basis, you will learn more about what various jobs are like and how the business functions. While on the job, you can observe the interaction between clients and cosmeticians, the interaction among coworkers, the different levels of management, and the general atmosphere. This can help you decide whether this is an area you would like to explore further.

EMPLOYERS

Approximately 30,000 skin care specialists are employed in the United States, and they work in a variety of business settings that provide beauty, fitness and health, or personal care services. They may work for salons, fitness centers, and spas, as well as at resorts, large hotels, and even cruise ships. Some work for cosmetology schools as instructors of esthetics. Those with experience and interest in having their own business may decide to run their own salon where they offer a variety of services.

STARTING OUT

After completing a cosmetician or cosmetology program and passing state board exams, you can seek a position as an entry-level cosmetician. Cosmeticians find their jobs through cosmetology schools—salons and spas often recruit directly from schools. Networking in the field is also a viable option for aspiring cosmeticians looking for good work. Reading trade publication classified ads is also a way to locate job openings. Salons and spas most often advertise open positions in newspaper classifieds. There are also some placement agencies that match cosmeticians with salons and spas looking for workers.

ADVANCEMENT

Upon first entering the field, a cosmetician will advance somewhat as he or she gains clientele. A large and steady clientele will translate into higher earnings and greater professional status.

Beyond the entry-level cosmetician, one can move up to director of cosmeticians (often called director of estheticians). Eventually a cosmetician or esthetician can become a spa or salon manager, then move up to spa or salon director. For many cosmeticians, an ultimate goal is to own a spa or salon. Some cosmeticians open their own salons after being certified and without having to work up the ranks of another spa or salon.

As an alternative to working in a salon or spa, some cosmeticians decide to teach in cosmetology schools or use their knowledge to demonstrate cosmetics and skin care products in department stores. Others become cosmetics sales representatives or start businesses as beauty consultants. Some cosmeticians work as examiners for state cosmetology boards.

EARNINGS

The U.S. Department of Labor, which groups cosmeticians with barbers, cosmetologists, and workers specializing in personal appearance services, reports that cosmeticians working full time had an annual median income of $23,340 (including tips) in 2005. Salaries ranged from less than $13,870 to more than $44,570. However, salaries for cosmeticians vary widely based on where they work, the method of payment (commission and tips only or commission, salary, and tips), and the clientele. Those working on commission and tips only will find their beginning incomes very low as they work to build a steady clientele. In addition, not every company provides health benefits, which adds extra costs for the entry-level cosmetician who may already be struggling. Some companies pay a salary plus commission, which obviously is better for the entry-level cosmetician who has yet to establish a clientele. Some salaries start at or near minimum wage. When tips are added in, cosmeticians may end up with yearly incomes somewhere between $13,000 and $15,000. Other base salaries may reach the lower to mid-$20,000s.

It is usually not until the cosmetician reaches a manager or director position that he or she will make upward of $50,000.

WORK ENVIRONMENT

Despite the fact that the field seems elite and glamorous, being a cosmetician is hard work. Through most of the day cosmeticians must work on their feet. Some days are relaxing while others are quite hectic. Cosmeticians and salon owners can easily work more than 40 hours per week. Weekend and lunch-hour time slots are often especially busy. According to Liza Wong, owner of Elite Skin Care, a salon in San Mateo, California, time management is the most difficult aspect of the job. "Cosmeticians must be flexible and willing to work late evenings and on weekends, around their clients' work schedules," says Wong.

On the positive side, it is a very social position. Cosmeticians see a variety of clients each day and perform a variety of services. They learn a lot from their clients—about their lives and their jobs.

OUTLOOK

Liza Wong predicts a big future for cosmeticians. "Americans are just starting to become aware of this field," Wong says. "These services, once only enjoyed by the rich, are becoming more affordable, and as baby boomers are trying to keep their youth and maintain their skin, there will be an increasing demand for skin care." The U.S. Department of Labor predicts that employment for cosmeticians will grow about as fast as the average for all other occupations through 2014. The growing popularity and affordability of day spas that offer full services should provide job opportunities for skin care specialists.

Spending for personal care services is considered by most people to be discretionary. Therefore, during hard economic times, people tend to visit cosmeticians less frequently, which reduces earnings. However, good cosmeticians are rarely laid off solely because of economic downturns.

FOR MORE INFORMATION

For industry news, a listing of accredited schools, and information on financial aid, contact

National Accrediting Commission of Cosmetology Arts and Sciences
4401 Ford Avenue, Suite 1300
Alexandria, VA 22302-1432
Tel: 703-600-7600
http://www.naccas.org

For industry news, contact

National Cosmetology Association
401 North Michigan Avenue, 22nd Floor
Chicago, IL 60611-4245
Tel: 312-527-6765
http://www.salonprofessionals.org

For information on membership, contact

Society of Dermatology SkinCare Specialists
484 Spring Avenue
Ridgewood, NJ 07450-4624
Tel: 201-670-4100
Email: sdssorg@aol.com
http://www.sdss.tv

For a listing of schools by state, check out the following Web site:

Beautyschool.com
http://www.beautyschool.com

For hair styling tips and techniques, job listings, and business advice, visit the following Web site:

Behind the Chair
http://www.behindthechair.com

Cosmetics Sales Representatives

OVERVIEW

Cosmetics sales representatives demonstrate and sell beauty-care products. Representatives may work from their homes as independent contractors, or they may work in retail establishments where they are employees of the store as well as employees of a cosmetics company.

HISTORY

As long ago as 3000 B.C., Egyptian priests prepared cosmetics for their kings. Their toiletries and other luxuries were entombed with them. When the tombs of these long-dead kings were excavated in modern times, vases of scented ointments were found, some still holding their fragrant contents. From the kings the use of cosmetics spread. Egyptian women painted their eyebrows, eyelids, and lashes black with the cosmetic kohl. Cosmetics were made of such naturally occurring substances as sesame oil, olive oil, floral and herbal scents, and other ingredients that were available to use in simple preparations. Henna was used to color the body or hair red. White lead or chalk was used to whiten the complexion. From the Middle East and the Mediterranean, the use of cosmetics spread through the Greeks to the Roman Empire and throughout Europe. The change from simple preparations of natural ingredients to the modern cosmetics industry began in France toward the end of the 19th century. The development of new techniques in manufacturing, packaging, advertising, and marketing has spread cosmetics—and their representatives—around the world.

QUICK FACTS

School Subjects
Business
Speech

Personal Skills
Artistic
Helping/teaching

Work Environment
Primarily indoors
One location with some
  travel

Minimum Education Level
Some postsecondary training

Salary Range
$13,590 to $30,000 to
  $150,000

Certification or Licensing
None available

Outlook
About as fast as the average

DOT
290

GOE
10.03.01

NOC
6411, 6421

O*NET-SOC
41-2031.00

THE JOB

Cosmetics sales representatives, or *beauty advisers,* help customers choose particular products appropriate to them. Cosmetics sales reps may consider the condition of the hair, the skin, and the coloring to recommend the cosmetics that will achieve the results desired by the customer. They also introduce the client to new products or techniques. These reps are usually women, but men are also welcome to pursue this career.

Beauty advisers who work in department or specialty stores usually work full time. They are hired by the store and the cosmetics company, both of which provide ongoing training and education. They display, restock, and sell products, attend meetings to learn about new campaigns for different seasons and holidays, attend training sessions, and meet the attendance and performance goals set by the store and by the cosmetics company.

Cosmetics sales representatives who work for such companies as Avon or Mary Kay are not employees but independent contractors who usually work part time. The goal remains to sell the products, and this job is appealing to those who want to supplement their incomes while keeping their hours flexible. Avon representatives usually distribute fliers or brochures within a specified territory. They take orders by phone or in person. Mary Kay also facilitates its salespeople to set up individual sales Web sites to sell their products. The orders are delivered to the rep, who then delivers them to the customer and collects the money. Mary Kay also uses fliers to advertise products and offers services such as skin care classes and facials.

REQUIREMENTS

High School

There are a number of classes you can take in high school to help prepare you for a sales career. Naturally, business classes can be beneficial. Knowledge of business practices and procedures will help you understand the industry. Speech and English classes as well as experience on a debating club will help you develop better communication skills. Also, you should consider taking psychology classes because selling requires an insightful knowledge of people and an ability to read the customer. Computer courses are useful since retail stores now use computerized record-keeping, and a course in accounting can help independent cosmetics sales representatives better manage their businesses.

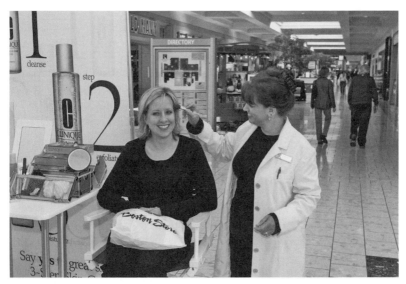

A cosmetics sales representative demonstrates makeup to a client. *(The Image Works)*

Postsecondary Training

Most of the beauty advisers who work for cosmetics companies in retail stores have college degrees or are working toward them. Business or marketing are possible majors for those in this field. Typically, some on-the-job training is involved for new employees at retail stores. There are no specific educational requirements for independent contractors, although some organizations, such as Mary Kay, offer materials and support to help their contractors learn about new products and improve their selling techniques. There is a minimum age requirement of 18 for virtually all positions in the field.

Other Requirements

An outgoing, enthusiastic person who enjoys talking with a variety of new people will enjoy this work. Good manners and being a team player are important. Someone with color blindness, asthma, or allergies—especially to perfumes—should probably not consider this line of work.

EXPLORING

There are entry-level jobs available nationwide. Talking to a cosmetics representative is as easy as picking up the telephone. Both Avon

Additional Opportunities in the Cosmetology Industry

The cosmetology industry offers a variety of career paths to people from all educational backgrounds. Here are just a few of the additional options not covered in this book:

- Accountants and auditors
- Advertising and promotions managers
- Association executives
- Beauty writers and editors
- Bookkeeping, accounting, and auditing clerks
- Chemical engineering technicians
- Chemical engineers
- Computer and Internet security specialists
- Computer programmers
- Computer software engineers
- Cosmetology teachers
- Customer service representatives
- Data entry and information processing workers
- Desktop publishers
- Graphic designers
- Janitors and cleaners
- Laboratory testing technicians
- Laborers
- Lawyers
- Manufacturing workers
- Models
- Office clerks
- Packaging designers
- Product demonstrators
- Public relations specialists
- Quality control engineers and technicians
- Research and development scientists
- Security workers
- Truck drivers
- Web developers
- Webmasters

and Mary Kay encourage and reward recruitment of other reps. Mary Kay requires the building of a team or unit of reps. Avon offers information on job opportunities at its Web site, http://avon company.com.

For jobs in stores, hiring is done by both the store and the cosmetics line, so it is possible to be hired by the cosmetics firm and placed in a store or to be hired by the store and recommended to the cosmetics firm. Personnel offices of stores can be reached by phone or in person for information and employment applications. Current representatives of those companies that are hiring are usually happy to talk to people who might be interested in joining their team or unit.

EMPLOYERS

Cosmetics sales representatives are usually self-employed, employed by department stores, or employed by cosmetics companies. It is easy to begin work as an independent contractor for companies such as Avon or Mary Kay. It may be difficult to do this exclusively, however, without supplemental income. Jobs with department stores offer better income security and benefits, but these are usually full-time positions requiring evenings and weekends. Since cosmetics sales continue to increase, as do retail sales in general, there will probably be an abundance of opportunities for those seeking regular employment with stores or cosmetics companies and for independent representatives alike. Unlike most jobs in the cosmetology industry, however, independent cosmetics sales representatives in remote or rural areas may do well due to a lack of department stores and retail establishments specializing in cosmetics.

STARTING OUT

Patrick Cummings became an Avon representative several years ago. He paid a one-time fee of $20 to begin. "My idea was to make a couple of extra bucks." Cummings owns a specialty meat market, and orders and deliveries come to him at the store; he believes that people don't want or expect to come to their homes anymore. Now his customers can pick up their lamb chops and their lipsticks at the same location.

To become a Mary Kay representative, it costs about $100 to buy the sample case. Many of the representatives find most of their customers at their full-time jobs and use cosmetics sales as a supplement to their incomes.

Many cosmetics sales representatives in retail stores start out as perfume spritzers hired by a cosmetics line, or they may be hired during a busy season by the store and then recommended to the cosmetics company.

ADVANCEMENT

Marianne Blokell began her career in cosmetics over 12 years ago. "I started as a freelance spritzer for Aramis perfume and was hired by Carson, Pirie, Scott, and Co. full time. I worked as a beauty adviser for Lancome at Carson's, was promoted to counter manager there, and now supervise Lancome counters for two stores." Two avenues of advancement are open to her. She can move up through Lancome from counter manager to account coordinator or account manager in charge of several stores, then to trainer/educator in charge of coaching, training, setting goals, or to account executive. Through Carson's, she can advance to a job as a buyer or a planner.

EARNINGS

The U.S. Department of Labor reports the median hourly wage, including commission, was $9.20 for all retail sales workers in 2005. A sales rep working full time at this pay rate would earn approximately $19,140 per year. Salaries ranged from less than $13,590 to more than $37,250. For cosmetics sales representatives working in stores, earnings vary because each retailer pays differently. Karen Broderick, an account manager for Lancome, offers some average figures. A beginning beauty adviser at Carson, Pirie, Scott, and Co. starts at $6.50 an hour plus 3 percent commission. After five years with a 5 percent raise annually, the average salary is $30,000 to $35,000 a year, which includes in-store incentives, commissions, and bonuses. As the representative rises from counter manager to account manager to account executive for a region, the compensation rises as high as $150,000.

For independent sales representatives, the earnings depend completely on commissions. If they sell nothing, they make nothing. Many independents make only about $100 a month, which is reasonable if they view the job as a supplement, not as their main income.

WORK ENVIRONMENT

Cosmetics representatives in retail stores usually work in attractive, climate-controlled settings. But the hours are long and they must be on their feet. There is a lot of bending and heavy boxes of stock to unload and display. They may not leave the sales floor except at specified times. Many stores have evening and Sunday hours, and breaks and lunch may go by the board in a crush of customers.

Independent contractors usually place orders and accept deliveries at home. They then deliver to their customers, who may be neighbors or coworkers at their primary place of employment.

OUTLOOK

The U.S. Department of Labor predicts that employment for all retail sales reps will grow about as fast as the average for all occupations through 2014. The job picture for cosmetics sales representatives, however, is somewhat mixed. While it is easy to get started in the field, most who choose it work only part time. Avon alone has more than 5 million representatives selling products in more than 100 countries. Mary Kay has more than 1.6 million independent beauty consultants in more than 30 countries. This is a good choice for people needing supplemental income or in transition, or young mothers who want to stay at home with their children, but most people need an additional job—their own or their spouse's—to provide enough income, health benefits, vacations, or just a day off. Growth in cosmetics companies seems to be international, directed toward opening up new markets in more and more countries; Avon, for example, has stores around the world, from Canada to Thailand, from Greece to Argentina, from Russia to Japan. However, Avon is now also selling cosmetics online, and it remains to be seen how this will affect the company's need for individual sales reps.

Retail selling is such a huge industry that there are always openings to replace those leaving the field, but the hours are long and the wages start out very low.

FOR MORE INFORMATION

For information on careers in cosmetics sales, contact or visit the following Web sites:

Avon Cosmetics
1251 Avenue of the Americas
New York, NY 10020-1104
Tel: 212-282-700
http://www.avon.com

Mary Kay Cosmetics
PO Box 799045
Dallas, TX 75379-9045
Tel: 800-627-9529
http://www.marykay.com

Cosmetics Shop Owners and Managers

OVERVIEW

Cosmetics shop owners are entrepreneurs who start or buy their own cosmetics businesses or franchise operations. They are responsible for all aspects of business operation, from planning and ordering merchandise (such as cosmetics, perfume, skin and hair care products, and beauty appliances and accessories) to overseeing day-to-day operations. *Cosmetics shop managers* are responsible for the profitable operation of cosmetics establishments. Their duties include hiring, training, and supervising other employees, maintaining the physical facilities, managing inventory, monitoring expenditures and receipts, and maintaining good public relations.

HISTORY

Growing public acceptance of the use of cosmetics; the development of new manufacturing and packaging techniques for cosmetics; and the emergence of the film industry (which needed makeup for its actors that would not crack or cake) created a demand for cosmetics in the early 20th century in the United States. In fact, U.S. cosmetics sales increased by 100 percent from 1900 to 1910. Around this time, cosmetics began to be sold in department stores. By the 1920s the rise of chain, or dime, stores allowed cosmetics to become available to the general public. After initial resistance, women's magazines began featuring ads for cosmetics by the late 1920s. In the following decades, new products and production techniques helped make the cosmetics industry one of the most successful industries in the United States. Managers were needed to supervise cosmetics store staff, and entrepreneurial-minded people were drawn to the opportunity to enter this exciting field as cosmetics store owners. Today, many brick-and-mortar cosmetics stores have a presence on the Internet, creating new opportunities for managers and entrepreneurs with expertise in Internet marketing and sales.

THE JOB

There are five major categories of job responsibilities within a cosmetics store: merchandising and buying, store operations, sales promotion and advertising, bookkeeping and accounting, and personnel supervision. Merchandising and buying determine the type and amount of actual goods to be sold—for example, the number of makeup lines to be featured and the number of units from each line that will be purchased. Store operations involve maintaining the building and providing for the movement of goods and personnel within the building. Sales promotion and advertising are the marketing methods used to inform customers and potential customers about the goods and services that are available—for example, a new line of skin care products or a special in-store appearance by a noted beauty expert. In bookkeeping and accounting, records are kept of payroll, taxes, and money spent and received. Personnel involves staffing the store with people who are trained and qualified to handle all the work that needs to be done.

The cosmetics shop owner must be aware of all aspects of the business operation so that he or she can make informed decisions. Specific duties of an individual owner depend on the size of the store and the number of employees.

In both large and small operations, an owner must keep up to date on product information, as well as on economic and technological conditions that may have an impact on business. This entails reading catalogs about product availability, checking current inventories and prices, and researching and implementing any technological advances that may make the operation more efficient. For example, an owner may decide to purchase data processing equipment to help with accounting functions, as well as to generate a mailing list to inform customers of special sales or new products.

Because of the risks involved in opening a business and the many economic and managerial demands put on individual owners, a desire to open a retail business should be combined with proper management skills, sufficient economic backing, and a good sense of what the public wants. The large majority of retail businesses fail because of a lack of managerial experience on the part of owners.

Franchise ownership, whereby an individual owner obtains a license to sell an existing company's goods or services, grew phenomenally during the 1980s. Franchise agreements enable the person who wants to open a business to receive expert advice from the sponsoring company about location, hiring and training of employees, arrangement of merchandise, display of goods, and record keeping. Some entrepreneurs, however, do not want to be limited to the product lines and other restrictions that accompany running a franchise store. Franchise operations also may fail, but their likelihood of success is greater than that of a totally independent retail store.

In larger cosmetics stores, a manager may supervise many of the operational, promotional, and personnel activities. The owner may plan the overall purpose and function of the store and hire a manager to oversee the day-to-day operations. Although cosmetics store managers are responsible for every phase of a store's operation, perhaps the most important responsibility of retail managers is hiring and training qualified employees. Managers then assign duties to employees, monitor their progress, promote employees, and increase salaries when appropriate. When an employee's performance is not satisfactory, a manager must find a way to improve the performance or, if necessary, fire him or her.

Cosmetics store managers should be good at working with all different kinds of people. Differences of opinion and personality clashes among employees are inevitable; therefore the manager must be able to restore good feelings among the staff. Managers often have to deal with upset customers, and must attempt to restore goodwill toward the store when customers are dissatisfied.

Cosmetics store managers keep accurate and up-to-date records of store inventory. When new merchandise arrives, the manager ensures items are recorded, priced, and displayed or shelved. They must know when stock is getting low and order new items in a timely manner.

Some managers are responsible for merchandise promotions and advertising. The manager may confer with an advertising agency representative to determine appropriate advertising methods for the store. The manager also may decide what products to put on sale for advertising purposes.

Many cosmetics stores have begun to sell their products and services on the Internet. *Internet cosmetics store managers and entrepreneurs* use the technology of the Internet to sell products or services. They may research the marketability of a product or service, decide on what product or service to sell, organize their business, and set up their storefront on the Web. Numerous small businesses owners who sell a limited number of products or a specific service have found the Internet a great place to begin their business venture because start-up costs may be less than for traditional businesses. Internet entrepreneurs run their own businesses. Internet cosmetics store managers are employed by Internet entrepreneurs and stores.

REQUIREMENTS

High School

A high school diploma is important in order to understand the basics of business ownership and management, though there are no specific educational or experiential requirements for this position. Course work in business administration is helpful, as is previous experience in the retail trade.

If you are interested in owning or managing a business, you should take courses in mathematics, business management, and in business-related subjects, such as accounting, typing, and computer science. In addition, pursue English and other courses that enhance your communications skills. Specific skill areas also should be developed. For example, if you want to open a cosmetics shop, you should learn as much about the cosmetics industry as possible.

Postsecondary Training

As the business environment gets more and more competitive, many people are opting for an academic degree as a way of getting more training. A bachelor's program emphasizing business communications, marketing, business law, business management, and accounting should be pursued. Some people choose to get a master's in business administration or other related graduate degree. There are also special business schools that offer a one- or two-year program in business management. Some correspondence schools also offer courses on how to plan and run a business.

Certification or Licensing

Cosmetics shop owners may need a business license to do business in some states. Individual states or communities may have zoning codes or other regulations specifying what type of business can be located in a particular area. Check with your state's chamber of commerce or department of revenue for more information on obtaining a license, or visit this Web site: http://www.sba.gov/hotlist/license.html.

Other Requirements

Whatever their experience and training, a cosmetics store owner needs a lot of energy, patience, and fortitude to overcome the slow times and other difficulties involved in running a business. Other important personal characteristics include maturity, creativity, and good business judgment. Business owners also should be able to motivate employees and delegate authority.

To be a successful cosmetics store manager, you should have good communication skills, enjoy working with and supervising people, and be willing to put in very long hours. Diplomacy often is necessary when creating schedules for workers and in disciplinary matters. There is a great deal of responsibility in retail management and such positions often are stressful. A calm disposition and ability to handle stress will serve you well.

EXPLORING

Working full or part time as a sales clerk or in some other capacity within a retail business is a good way to learn about the responsibilities of operating and managing a business. Talking with owners of small shops (especially those that specialize in cosmetics) is also helpful, as is reading periodicals, such as *Cosmetic World* magazine (http://www.cosmeticworld.com), that cover the cosmetics industry.

Most communities have a chamber of commerce whose members usually will be glad to share their insights into the career of a retail business owner and manager. The Small Business Administration, an agency of the U.S. government, is another possible source of information.

EMPLOYERS

Cosmetics shop owners may own their own small businesses or become franchise owners. Cosmetics store managers work for large department stores such as Nordstrom, Neiman Marcus, and Macy's; stand-alone cosmetics store chains such as Sephora, Aveda, Lush, ULTA, MAC Cosmetics, and Bare Escentuals; and for small business owners. Other managers may work for Internet-based cosmetics stores.

STARTING OUT

Few people start their career as an owner. Many start as a manager or in some other position within a retail business. While developing managerial skills or while pursuing a college degree or other relevant training, you should decide what type of business you would like to own. Many people decide to buy an existing business because it already has a proven track record and because banks and other lending institutions often are more likely to loan money to an existing facility. A retail business owner should anticipate having at least 50 percent of the money needed to start or buy a business. Some people find it helpful to have one or more partners in a business venture.

Owning a franchise is another way of starting a business without a large capital investment, as franchise agreements often involve some assistance in planning and start-up costs. Franchise operations, however, are not necessarily less expensive to run than a totally independent business.

Many new college graduates are able to find managerial positions through their school's career services office. Some of the large retail chains recruit on college campuses.

Not all cosmetics store managers, however, are college graduates. Many store managers are promoted to their positions from jobs of less responsibility within their organization. Some may be in the retail industry for more than a dozen years before being promoted. Those with more education often receive promotions faster.

Regardless of educational background, people who are interested in the retail cosmetics industry should consider working in a retail store at least part time or during the summer. Although there may not be an opening when the application is made, there often is a high turnover of employees in retail management, and vacancies occur from time to time.

ADVANCEMENT

Because an owner is by definition the boss, there are limited opportunities for advancement. Advancement often takes the form of expansion of an existing business, leading to increased earnings and prestige. Expanding a business also can entail added risk, as it involves increasing operational costs. A successful franchise owner may be offered an additional franchise location or an executive position at the corporate headquarters. A small number of successful independent business owners choose to franchise their business operations in different areas. Some owners become part-time consultants, while others teach a course at a college or university or in an adult education program. This teaching often is done not only for the financial rewards but also as a way of helping others investigate the option of retail ownership.

Advancement opportunities for cosmetics store managers vary according to the size of the store, where the store is located, and the individual's work experience and educational background.

A store manager who works for a large cosmetics store chain, for example, may be given responsibility for a number of stores in a given area or region or transferred to a larger store in another city. Willingness to relocate may increase an employee's promotional opportunities.

Some managers decide to open their own stores after they have acquired enough experience in the cosmetics industry. After working as a retail manager for the cosmetics department at Nordstrom, for example, a person may decide to open a small store in an up-and-coming neighborhood near their home.

EARNINGS

Earnings for cosmetics store owners vary widely and are greatly influenced by the ability of the individual owner and existing economic conditions. Some cosmetics store owners may earn less than $15,000 a year, while the most successful owners earn $100,000 or more.

Salaries for cosmetics store managers depend on the size of the store, the responsibilities of the job, types of products and services that are sold, and the number of customers served. According to the U.S. Department of Labor, median annual earnings of supervisors of retail sales workers, including commission, were $32,840 in 2005. Salaries ranged from less than $20,500 to more than $57,420 per year. Managers who oversee an entire region for a retail chain can earn more than $100,000.

In addition to a salary, some stores offer their managers special bonuses, or commissions, which are typically connected to the store's performance. Many stores also offer employee discounts on store merchandise and services.

WORK ENVIRONMENT

Cosmetics store owners and managers generally work in pleasant surroundings. Even so, these are demanding occupations, with owners and managers often working six or seven days a week. Working more than 60 hours a week is not unusual, especially during the holiday season and other busy times. Owners and managers often stay in the store throughout the day, spending much of the time on their feet.

OUTLOOK

The cosmetics industry is one of the most successful industries in the United States, with sales exceeding $32 billion in 2005—an increase of nearly $8 billion since 2000. Despite this strong growth, the industry is extremely competitive, and many businesses—especially smaller cosmetics stores—fail each year. The weakening of consumer confidence, increased competition from other retailers and direct-marketers, and the growth of Internet businesses are just some of the issues cosmetics store owners will face in the next decade.

Employment of retail managers (including cosmetics store managers) is expected to grow more slowly than the average for all occupations through 2014, according to the U.S. Department of Labor. Although retailers have reduced their management staff to cut costs and make operations more efficient, there still are good opportunities in retailing. Internet stores and e-commerce ventures will present many new opportunities for cosmetics store managers, for example. However, competition for all jobs will probably continue to increase, and computerized systems for inventory control may reduce the need for some managers. Applicants with the best educational backgrounds and work experience will have the best chances of finding jobs. There will always be a need for cosmetics store managers, however, as long as retail stores exist. Retail manager positions are rarely affected by corporate restructuring at retail headquarters; this has a greater impact on home office staff.

FOR MORE INFORMATION

The following foundation conducts research and analysis of women-owned businesses.

Center for Women's Business Research
1411 K Street, NW, Suite 1350
Washington, DC 20005-3407
Tel: 202-638-3060
Email: info@womensbusinessresearch.org
http://www.womensbusinessresearch.org

For information on executive-level career opportunities in the cosmetics industry, contact

Cosmetic Executive Women
286 Madison Avenue, 19th Floor
New York, NY 10017-6302

Tel: 212-685-5955
Email: cew@cew.org
http://cew.org/about/contact

To read Career Opportunities in the Cosmetic, Toiletry, and Fragrance Industry, *visit the following Web site:*
The Cosmetic, Toiletry, and Fragrance Association
1101 17th Street, NW, Suite 300
Washington, DC 20036-4702
Tel: 202-331-1770
http://www.ctfa.org

For materials on educational programs in the retail industry, contact
National Retail Federation
325 Seventh Street, NW, Suite 1100
Washington, DC 20004-2818
Tel: 800-673-4692
http://www.nrf.com

For information on jobs in retail, contact
Retail Industry Leaders Association
1700 North Moore Street, Suite 2250
Arlington, VA 22209-1933
Tel: 703-841-2300
http://www.retail-leaders.org

For a business starter packet with information about its loan program and services, and basic facts about starting a business, contact
U.S. Small Business Administration
Tel: 800-827-5722
Email: answerdesk@sba.gov
http://www.sbaonline.sba.gov

Visit the following Web sites for information on the cosmetics industry:
CosmeticIndustry.com
http://www.cosmeticindustry.com

CosmeticNews.com
http://www.cosmeticnews.com

Cosmetic Surgeons

OVERVIEW

Cosmetic surgeons (also known as *plastic surgeons* and *esthetic surgeons*) are medical doctors who specialize in surgeries to correct disfigurement and/or improve physical appearance. Though the terms cosmetic and plastic surgery are often used interchangeably, cosmetic surgery usually means procedures performed to reshape normal structures of the body to improve the patient's appearance. Plastic surgery generally refers to reconstructive surgeries performed on abnormal structures of the body caused by birth defects, developmental abnormalities, trauma, injury, infection, tumors, or disease.

HISTORY

Contrary to popular belief, cosmetic surgery is not a recent development. Although the increase in the popularity of certain cosmetic procedures is a relatively new trend, surgeons have been correcting human disfigurement since 3400 B.C., when Egyptian healers performed cosmetic operations on the face, feet, and arms. Another ancient tie can be found in the profession's own name. The *plastic* in plastic surgery does not mean "artificial." Rather, plastic surgery derives its name from the ancient Greek word *plastikos*, which meant to mold or give form. In fact, the modern day "nose job," which Hollywood celebrities seem to favor, likely got its start in ancient India, although the procedures done at that time were for reconstructive rather than strictly cosmetic purposes. By 800 B.C., physicians in India were using skin grafts (a process that transfers healthy skin from one part of the body to another for the purpose of replacing damaged or lost skin) to perform reconstructive work for facial injuries.

Cosmetic surgery changed little during the Dark Ages but began to develop again in the 1700s, when British surgeons introduced to Europe techniques they had seen in India. Further improvement in skin grafting techniques continued, but progress was slow until the early 1900s.

Before World War I, the profession evolved slowly in North America as well. Virginian Dr. John Peter Mettauer performed the first cleft palate operation in the New World in 1827 with instruments he designed himself. With the advent of world war, physicians were challenged to find ways to treat extensive facial and head injuries never before seen, such as shattered jaws and gaping skull wounds.

It was not until the late 1930s that the American Board of Surgeons, the medical certifying organization of the time, established a specialty board to certify cosmetic surgeons—the American Board of Plastic Surgery—with its own standards and specialized training. Prior to the establishment of this board, many physicians who performed reconstructive surgeries were from other specialties related to cosmetic surgery.

New techniques developed in the 1950s included internal wiring for facial fractures and rotation flaps for skin deformities. In the 1960s, the scope of procedures performed by surgeons widened as the public became more informed. Cosmetic procedures became more popular. Silicone was initially used to treat skin imperfections and was first used as a breast implant device in 1962. The 1980s saw plastic surgeons expand their efforts to bring information to the public, and in the 1990s, the profession focused efforts on having reconstructive procedures covered under health plans.

Despite the many advances, the field is still evolving. Today, researchers are trying to unlock the secrets of the growth-factor environment of the womb, where scarless healing takes place, in order to apply the technique to wounds of children and adults.

THE JOB

Doctors, especially specialists such as cosmetic surgeons, generally work long hours. Surgeries of all types demand strict attention to detail, and cosmetic surgeries in which the emphasis is on the quality of the patient's appearance can be especially challenging. Still, the profession offers high earnings and personal rewards. Physicians tend to be people who thrive on challenge and are willing to devote a lot of time to their careers.

Of course, cosmetic surgeons do not spend all their working hours in surgery. Daily tasks include patient consultation and record keeping, among other duties. Also, no matter what setting a surgeon practices in, he or she is likely to have administrative duties as well. Surgeons in private practice have an office to manage with duties ranging from hiring employees to marketing the practice to overseeing upkeep of the office. Surgeons who work in a hospital's plastic surgery department have commitments to the hospital outside of performing surgeries and seeing patients. For example, cosmetic surgeons frequently are required to provide general hospital emergency room coverage and split up this task with the other surgeons.

Dr. Richard Maloney, a cosmetic surgeon who practices at the Aesthetic Surgery Center in Naples, Florida, estimates he spends about 60 percent of his time in surgery. Other time is spent on patient visits, follow-up, initial consultations, and emergency room coverage. Maloney acknowledges that many in the field of medicine push themselves to work days as long as 16 hours, seven days a week, but he said that doctors can and should decide how much time they want to devote to work and follow that decision.

"In the field of medicine, the urge to take on a workload to prove yourself is great. I think the average workweek can be as much as you want it to be," Maloney said. In practice for 19 years, Maloney said he has found 10-hour days provide a good balance between his personal and professional life.

Today's cosmetic surgeons perform a wider range of procedures than their counterparts did only a few decades ago. Previously, the profession focused on reconstructive surgeries, with a few surgeons catering to those who could afford cosmetic procedures. Today, cosmetic surgeries are no longer performed on just celebrities or the wealthy. The public has become familiar with terms such as *liposuction* (removal of unwanted fatty deposits), *implants*, and *facelift* because those procedures have become more accessible to the general population. According to the American Society of Plastic Surgeons (ASPS), the top five cosmetic procedures in 2006 were liposuction, nose reshaping, breast augmentation, eyelid surgery, and tummy tuck. And as cosmetic surgery becomes more commonplace, an increasing number of men are having it done. Nose reshaping, hair transplants, liposuction, and eyelid surgery are some of the most popular procedures among men, according to the ASPS. Today's cosmetic surgeons perform more strictly cosmetic procedures than the average cosmetic surgeon did even a decade ago. Of course, a surgeon can still choose to specialize in reconstructive surgery, but trends indicate growth in the field is with cosmetic procedures.

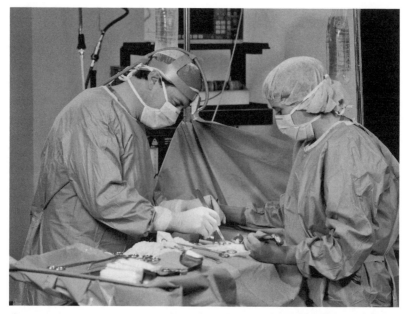

Cosmetic surgeons must be highly disciplined, able to perform complex tasks with a high degree of accuracy, and work as a member of a team. *(Corbis)*

It should be noted, however, that more reconstructive procedures remain important. The ASPS reports that 94 percent of its members perform cosmetic surgery and 89 percent perform reconstructive surgery.

There are different settings in which a cosmetic surgeon may work. Three arrangements are common. The first is private practice, in which the surgeon is the sole physician in a practice with his or her own staff. The physician performs surgeries either in his or her own clinic or at a hospital where he or she has privileges. The second is group practice, in which a surgeon is part of a group of cosmetic surgeons or other related specialists who market their services together. Group practice surgeons may also perform surgeries in their own clinic or at a hospital. The third common arrangement is working in hospital departments, where a surgeon is a member of a hospital's plastic surgery department. A less common career path for cosmetic surgeons who have considerable surgical experience are professorships at academic institutions or teaching hospitals.

Because plastic surgery is a highly specialized field, plastic surgeons generally work in urban areas, both large and small. Most rural areas don't have enough patients to create a reasonable demand.

According to ASPS estimates, more than half of its approximately 6,000 members work in large metropolitan areas.

REQUIREMENTS

High School

If you want to pursue a career in medicine, prepare yourself by learning the self-discipline to concentrate on schoolwork in high school in order to achieve the grades necessary to gain entrance to a good undergraduate program. Performing well at the college level can help you compete for slots in medical school. Start working hard in high school by taking college preparatory classes such as mathematics (including algebra and geometry) and sciences (including biology, chemistry, and physics). Also, consider taking a foreign language. Many college programs have foreign language requirements, and a familiarity with some foreign languages may help you with your medical studies later on. Finally, don't forget to take English courses. These classes will help you develop your research and writing skills—two skills that will be essential to you in your career.

In addition, check out school clubs and civic organizations that offer volunteer opportunities for students in places like local hospitals or nursing homes. In addition to the experience you will get by volunteering, you will also have the opportunity to establish valuable relationships with people who work in the health care field. Clubs such as Kiwanis, Rotary, and Lions often count community leaders such as doctors, hospital administrators, and other health care professionals among their members. Many of these clubs have charter clubs in high schools, and student members have regular contact with these community leaders.

Postsecondary Training

Training to become a doctor is a rigorous, lengthy process. After high school, students pursuing a career in medicine can expect to spend 11 to 16 years in school and training before they can practice medicine. Requirements include four years of undergraduate school, four years of medical school, and three to eight years of residency. Not all students who apply to medical school are accepted, and many go on to other careers in the field of medicine. Entry to medical school is very competitive, and prospective students must show they possess exceptional academic abilities. Medical schools also consider character, personality, leadership qualities, and participation in extracurricular activities when deciding whether to accept a student.

The minimum education requirement for entry to a medical school is three years of college, although most applicants have at least a bachelor's degree and many have advanced degrees. Undergraduate degrees obtained by medical school applicants vary, but many have degrees in mathematics, engineering, or sciences such as biology, or in premed. Premedical students complete courses in physics, biology, mathematics, English, and inorganic and organic chemistry. Some students also volunteer at local hospitals or clinics to gain practical experience. This volunteer experience will weigh in a student's favor on competitive medical school applications.

Junior and senior years in undergraduate school for students planning to go on to medical school are very busy years. In addition to keeping up with their studies, junior and senior undergraduates often spend much of their time researching medical school programs, volunteering, or gaining other experience that could be helpful on a medical school application. Students should keep in mind that acceptance to medical school is highly competitive. At a top medical school in the nation, for example, the class of 2000 consisted of 104 men and 67 women selected from 8,639 applicants. The students accepted had an average grade point average of 3.5 on a 4.0 scale. Medical school lasts four years, in addition to the four years a student has already put in at the undergraduate level, so those who want to pursue a medical career should be prepared to commit many years to being a student. All physicians, whether or not they plan to specialize in a field such as cosmetic surgery, must complete additional training. Specialty training, depending on the field, varies from three to eight years. Traditionally, medical school graduates spend their first graduate year in a hospital internship. This first year of training following medical school is called the PGY-1, during which graduates work long hours to learn about assuming the responsibility for care of patients in the role of a physician.

After the first year, students are generally matched up into an internship program known as a residency program. It is during residency that physicians-in-training are introduced to their chosen specialties. Residents work under physicians who are specialists in their chosen fields at a teaching hospital. Medical school graduates must apply to residency programs by ranking their preferences for different hospitals. Independent agencies, such as the National Resident Matching Program (http://www.nrmp.org), match the student's preferences with the programs for which they are qualified. Accepted residency programs are accredited by the Accreditation Council for Graduate Medical Education (http://www.acgme.org/acWebsite/home/home.asp).

Certification or Licensing

All 50 states require physicians be licensed to practice. Certification by one of the 24 certifying boards recognized by the American Board of Medical Specialties is not a legal requirement. Many physicians choose to become certified in their field because certification enables the public to identify practitioners who have met a standard of training and experience beyond the level required for licensure. As consumers become more informed and health care becomes more market-driven, physicians who are board certified are expected to be in greater demand. Many patient advocate groups and patient information sources urge patients to choose physicians who are board certified.

In order to receive certification from the American Board of Plastic Surgery (ABPS), a candidate must have successfully completed the approved residency program in plastic surgery. The plastic and reconstructive surgeon then applies to the ABPS and, once the application is approved, takes the qualifying written examination. After passing the written examination, the applicant must then pass the oral examination.

In order to become certified, the plastic and reconstructive surgeon must also practice the specialty of plastic surgery for two years. The candidate can take the written examination anytime during the two years of practice, but the oral examination cannot be taken before the candidate has finished the two-year practice requirement.

The American Board of Cosmetic Surgery certifies physicians in the following areas: general cosmetic surgery, facial cosmetic surgery, and dermatologic cosmetic surgery. Requirements vary slightly for each area, but basic requirements include a one- or two-year fellowship in an approved program; proof of hospital operating room privileges; proof of a valid medical license; and certification by one of the following boards recognized by the American Board of Medical Specialties, the Bureau of Osteopathic Specialists of the American Osteopathic Association, or the Royal College of Physicians and Surgeons of Canada: Plastic and Reconstructive Surgery, Otolaryngology, General Surgery, Ophthalmology (with completion of an American Society of Ophthalmic Plastic and Reconstructive Surgery–approved Oculoplastic fellowship), or Dermatology.

Other Requirements

The field of medicine demands highly disciplined individuals who can perform complex tasks with a high degree of accuracy. Cosmetic surgery requires skill and artistry, as well as these talents, according to Dr. Richard Maloney. "It takes a fastidious person, but not to a fault," says Dr. Maloney. "There are a lot of steps to

Cosmetic Surgery Facts, 2006

- Nearly $11.5 billion was spent on cosmetic surgery.
- More than 11 million cosmetic surgery procedures were performed—an increase of 7 percent from 2005.
- Approximately 1.9 million surgical cosmetic procedures were performed—an increase of 2 percent from 2005. Top five procedures: breast augmentation, nose reshaping, liposuction, eyelid surgery, and tummy tuck.
- About 9.1 million minimally invasive cosmetic procedures were performed—an increase of 8 percent from 2005. Top five procedures: botox, chemical peel, laser hair removal, microdermabrasion, and hyaluronic acid.
- Approximately 5.3 million reconstructive surgical procedures were performed—a decrease of 3 percent from 2005. Top five procedures: tumor removal, laceration repair, scar revision, hand surgery, and breast reduction.

Source: American Society of Plastic Surgeons

the surgical procedures a plastic surgeon performs. Each must be properly executed; if it's not, it amplifies the error in the next step, and so on. Plastic surgeons do well if they enjoy growing and generating results," he adds. Hard work, self-confidence, and dedication are also vital. "It's a very rewarding line of work, but probably the biggest drawback is all of the work and years of schooling it takes to get to this point. But if students are really interested, they should follow their interests and take each hurdle as it comes."

Medicine also requires its successful professionals to have strong people skills in addition to knowledge and discipline. People are the "objects of the trade" for physicians, and communication skills and the ability to empathize with a wide variety of people is essential. The ability to work as part of a team is also important. A cosmetic surgeon performs surgeries and therefore depends on a surgical team to assist in surgery. The cosmetic surgeon must be able to communicate and work well with colleagues as well as patients.

EXPLORING

At the high school and undergraduate levels, you can begin to learn about the field of medicine by volunteering at hospitals, nursing homes, or clinics. By working in these settings you will not only have the opportunity to gauge how much you enjoy this type of work, but you will also have the chance to be around professionals in the field.

Another way you can explore is by talking to medical professionals, for example, interviewing one for a term paper or other school project. Or you may simply tell a doctor you know that you are interested in his or her profession and request an informational interview. Come to the interview prepared to ask questions. Ask the doctor how he or she got started in the field. What does he or she like most about the job, and what least? What were the years of school like? People are often happy to talk about their jobs if you show a sincere interest, and you may even discover a mentor in this way.

One national organization, the National Youth Leadership Forum (NYLF), offers an annual forum for high school students interested in a career in medicine. This 10-day forum, offered several times during the summer in various cities throughout the United States, gives students an opportunity to gain hands-on experience in medicine by visiting medical schools, research facilities, and hospitals and talking to people in various stages of the medical career path, from first-year medical students to practicing physicians. The curriculum in the NYLF medical forum covers a broad range of topics in medicine, including educational requirements, career options, clinical practice, and current issues facing the profession. Forums are open to juniors and seniors with 3.3 or above grade point averages. Teachers and guidance counselors recommend students accepted for forums. Students may ask about the program at their school or contact the organization themselves. Tuition fees and travel expenses apply, as the NYLF is a nonprofit organization, but many students are able to find sponsors in their community.

EMPLOYERS

When a cosmetic surgeon works in private practice, either alone or with a group of other specialists, the surgeon is essentially self-employed and running his or her own business. Surgeons may also work for hospitals, health maintenance organizations (HMOs), or the government, such as at the U.S. Department of Veterans Affairs. In addition, universities employ a number of surgeons in academic positions.

STARTING OUT

All physicians are required to have a medical degree. Beyond that, there are many options for entering various specialties. Four years of residency training is required of all surgeons certified by the American Board of Cosmetic Surgery (ABCS). However, the nature of that residency training, and to some extent, the location, may be up to the individual.

Many cosmetic surgeons participate in residency programs and take the exam to become board certified in cosmetic surgery. The ABCS offers certification opportunities to specialists in other fields, including general surgery, gynecology, otolaryngology, oral and maxillofacial surgery, dermatology, and ophthalmology. These specialties are related to many specific plastic surgery procedures and provide a different avenue of entering the field. Physicians certified in these fields are generally limited to performing surgeries in their specialty areas (for example, dermatologists would perform burn repair surgery or other graft surgery, but they are not likely to perform liposuction).

ADVANCEMENT

Once physicians become licensed as cosmetic surgeons, their opportunities for advancement are largely up to them. For many cosmetic surgeons, becoming board certified by the American Board of Cosmetic Surgeons is a first step in advancing their careers. As consumers become more informed about their options for cosmetic surgery, cosmetic surgeons with added credentials such as board certifications are likely to be in higher demand. Many associations, such as the American Society of Plastic Surgeons (ASPS), offer a screening service for consumers, enabling them to check a cosmetic surgeon's qualifications when choosing a surgeon.

Any further training a cosmetic surgeon undergoes, such as the additional years of residency required to learn a subspecialty, will increase his or her earnings.

Cosmetic surgeons who are part of a hospital's cosmetic surgery department may have opportunities for advancement within their department or to a higher position at other hospitals. Generally, cosmetic surgeons who are promoted within their departments have years of experience. Some do research outside of their surgery duties and publish their works in medical journals. Others teach cosmetic surgery at universities or become part of the staff to teach residents in a teaching hospital.

Some cosmetic surgeons with years of experience go on to chair cosmetic surgery departments at major hospitals or universities, spending less time on cosmetic surgery and more time on administrative duties and research.

EARNINGS

It takes many years of training to become a doctor, but earnings are among the highest of any occupation. For doctors, more so than for other fields, the number of years of training directly correlates with the earnings level. Specialists, such as cosmetic surgeons, generally earn more money than general practitioners. The more specialized the field, the higher the earnings.

The latest data available from the U.S. Department of Labor notes that surgeons (of all types) had a mean income of $177,690 in 2005. According to *Medical Economics,* a magazine for medical professionals, plastic surgeons in office-based private practice had a median annual gross income of $1 million in 2005. After expenses, their median income was $400,000. According to the recruitment firm Physicans Search (http://www.physicianssearch.com), responses to its Physician Compensation Survey show that plastic surgeons with three-plus years experience averaged $306,047 annually in 2007. The lowest paid respondent specializing in plastic surgery earned $196,711 per year, and the highest paid had an annual income of $411,500.

Cosmetic surgeons, and physicians in general, enjoy generous health care benefits. Other benefits may include recruitment bonuses, pay for continuing education, and forgiveness of school loans. Although they work long hours throughout the year, physicians are often granted several weeks' paid vacation and other leave time as relief from the demanding jobs they have.

WORK ENVIRONMENT

There are advantages to working in the different work arrangements available to a plastic surgeon (private practice, group practice, hospital department, or government or academic setting). A surgeon's preference may depend on how he or she works with others, as well as geographic location. Hospital plastic surgery departments are usually structured with department chairs and supervisors. Although a hospital setting generally means more rules for a physician to work under, it also offers the advantage of a structured environment, less individual financial risk, and the ability to share information and learn from colleagues daily. Those who prefer to be their own boss generally assume greater risk in a private or group practice, as does any small-business owner. Plastic surgeons in private or group practice should be business oriented or hire someone who can tend to marketing, accounting, and personnel concerns.

As with many specialists, cosmetic surgeons generally practice in big cities or smaller urban areas, but not rural areas. Big city settings generally bring advantages such as proximity to colleagues and shorter traveling distance to seminars and the hours of continuing education required of board-certified surgeons every year. Urban life brings increased cultural and recreational opportunities, but it can also mean headaches such as traffic and a higher cost of living.

Cosmetic surgeons, compared with other specialists, are not in frequent contact with contagious disease or hazardous chemicals. Some cosmetic procedures require the use of chemicals for injections or surface application, but surgeons are well trained and well regulated in their use of these materials.

The profession is not without its opportunities for service to humanity, but it is often these situations that put a cosmetic surgeon in contact with some dangers. Areas where people suffer from contagious disease and political violence in remote parts of developing countries are often the areas of greatest need for reconstructive surgeries. A program affiliated with the American Society of Plastic Surgeons, the Reconstructive Surgeons Volunteer Program, sends U.S. surgeons to such areas. Surgeons perform vital work there on people who had no hope of getting help from their own country, but the surgeons' accommodations often include only the bare essentials. Extreme weather, insects, and the sound of shots being fired in the distance are situations some surgeons have encountered.

OUTLOOK

According to the U.S. Department of Labor, the demand for physicians and surgeons is expected to grow faster than the average for all occupations through 2014. Because of population trends that include a rapidly aging population, physicians who meet the needs of older Americans can expect to see a steady demand for their services. Cosmetic surgeons, who treat conditions associated with aging and help older people maintain a youthful appearance, can be counted among medical specialists who will be in strong demand by the aging baby boomer population.

According to statistics compiled by the ASPS, the market for these surgeons is large: In 2006, there were approximately 5.3 million reconstructive procedures done, approximately 1.9 million major cosmetic surgeries, and approximately 9.1 million "minimally invasive" cosmetic procedures. Men make up a growing clientele, accounting for 9 percent of the cosmetic surgery performed in 2006.

FOR MORE INFORMATION

To *learn about cosmetic procedures and recent statistics, contact*
American Academy of Cosmetic Surgery
737 North Michigan Avenue, Suite 2100
Chicago, IL 60611-5405
Tel: 312-981-6760
http://www.cosmeticsurgery.org

Among this foundation's goals are promoting high standards of training, conferring scholarships, and increasing public education in plastic surgery matters.
American Society of Plastic Surgeons and The Plastic Surgery
    Educational Foundation
444 East Algonquin Road
Arlington Heights, IL 60005-4654
Tel: 847-228-9900
http://www.plasticsurgery.org

This association is devoted to providing information about medical schools in the United States.
Association of American Medical Colleges
2450 N Street, NW
Washington, DC 20037-1126
Tel: 202-828-0400
http://www.aamc.org

This organization offers career programs to high school students interested in the medical profession. Forums are offered in Atlanta, Boston, Chicago, Houston-Galveston, Los Angeles, Philadelphia, Phoenix, San Francisco, and Washington, D.C. Visit its Web site for information on schedule dates.
National Youth Leadership Forum
888 16th Street, NW, Suite 800
Washington, DC 20006-4103
Tel: 703-584-9315
Email: medicine_adm@nylf.org
http://www.nylf.org

Cosmetologists

OVERVIEW

Cosmetologists practice hair-care skills (including washing, cutting, coloring, perming, and applying various conditioning treatments), esthetics (performing skin care treatments), and nail care (grooming of hands and feet). Barbers are not cosmetologists; they undergo separate training and licensing procedures. There are approximately 339,000 cosmetologists, hairdressers, and hairstylists employed in the United States.

HISTORY

The history of the profession of cosmetology begins with barbering (the Latin *barba* means beard), one of the oldest trades, described by writers in ancient Greece. Relics of rudimentary razors date to the Bronze Age, and drawings of people in early Chinese and Egyptian cultures show men with shaved heads, indicating the existence of a barbering profession.

Barbers often did more than hair care. The treatment of illnesses by bloodletting, a task originally performed by monks, was passed along to barbers in 1163 by the papacy. Although trained physicians were already established at this time, they supported and encouraged the use of barbers for routine medical tasks, such as the treatment of wounds and abscesses. From the 12th century to the 18th century, barbers were known as barber-surgeons. They performed medical and surgical services, such as extracting teeth, treating disease, and cauterizing wounds.

Barbers began to organize and form guilds in the 14th century. A barbers' guild was formed in France in 1361. In 1383, the

QUICK FACTS

School Subjects
Art
Business
Speech

Personal Skills
Artistic
Mechanical/manipulative

Work Environment
Primarily indoors
Primarily one location

Minimum Education Level
Some postsecondary training

Salary Range
$13,400 to $20,610 to $37,380+

Certification or Licensing
Required by all states

Outlook
About as fast as the average

DOT
332

GOE
11.04.01

NOC
6271

O*NET-SOC
39-5012.00

barber of the king of France was decreed to be the head of that guild. The Barbers of London was established as a trade guild in 1462. Barbers distinguished themselves from surgeons and physicians by their titles. Barbers, who were trained through apprenticeships, were referred to as doctors of the short robe; university-trained doctors were doctors of the long robe. In England, during the first part of the 16th century, laws were established to limit the medical activities of barbers. They were allowed to let blood and perform tooth extractions only, while surgeons were banned from performing activities relegated to barbers, such as shaving.

Surgeons separated from the barbers' guild in England and in 1800 established their own guild, the Royal College of Surgeons. Laws were passed to restrict the activities of barbers to nonmedical practices. Barbers continued to be trained through apprenticeships until the establishment of barber training schools at the beginning of the 20th century.

Women did not begin to patronize barbershops until the 1920s. The *bob*, a hairstyle in which women cut their hair just below the ears, became popular at that time. Until that time, women usually wore their hair long. In the 1920s, shorter styles for women became acceptable and women began to go to barbers for cutting and styling. This opened the door for women to join the profession, and many began training to work with women's hairstyles.

Today, women and a growing number of men patronize hair salons or beauty shops to have their hair cut, styled, and colored. The barbershop, on the other hand, remains largely the domain of men.

Until the 1920s, *beauticians* (as they were commonly known) performed their services in their clients' homes. The beauty salons and shops now so prevalent have emerged as public establishments in more recent years. In the United States—as in many other countries—the cosmetology business is among the largest of the personal service industries.

THE JOB

Cosmetology uses hair as a medium to sculpt, perm, color, or design to create a fashion attitude. Cosmetologists, also known as *hairstylists*, perform all of these tasks as well as provide other services, such as deep conditioning treatments, special-occasion long-hair designs, and a variety of hair-addition techniques.

A licensed hairstylist can perform the hair services noted above and also is trained and licensed to do the basics of esthetics and nail technology. To specialize in esthetics or nail technology, additional

A cosmetologist applies color highlights to a client's hair. *(The Image Works)*

courses are taken in each of these disciplines—or someone can study just esthetics or just nail technology and get a license in either or both of these areas.

Cosmetology schools teach some aspects of human physiology and anatomy, including the bone structure of the head and some elementary facts about the nervous system, in addition to hair skills. Some schools have now added psychology-related courses, dealing with people skills and communications.

Hairstylists may be employed in shops that have as few as one or two employees, or as many as 20 or more. They may work in privately owned salons or in a salon that is part of a large or small chain of beauty shops. They may work in hotels, department stores, hospitals, nursing homes, resort areas, or on cruise ships. In recent years, a number of hair professionals—especially in big cities—have gone to work in larger facilities, sometimes known as spas or institutes, which offer a variety of health and beauty services. One such business, for example, offers complete hair design/treatment/color services; manicures and pedicures; makeup; bridal services; spa services including different kinds of facials (thermal mask, antiaging, acne treatment), body treatments (exfoliating sea salt glow, herbal body wrap), scalp treatments, hydrotherapy water treatments, massage therapy, eyebrow/eyelash tweezing and tinting, and hair-removal treatments for all parts of the body; a fashion boutique; and even a wellness center staffed with board-certified physicians.

Those who operate their own shops must also take care of the details of business operations. Bills must be paid, orders placed, invoices and supplies checked, equipment serviced, and records and books kept. The selection, hiring, and termination of other workers are also the owner's responsibility. Like other responsible business people, shop and salon owners are likely to be asked to participate in civic and community projects and activities.

Some stylists work for cosmetic/hair product companies. Sean Woodyard, for instance, in addition to being employed as a stylist at a big-city salon, teaches hair coloring for a major national cosmetics/hair care company. When the company introduces a new product or sells an existing product to a new salon, the company hires hair professionals as "freelance educators" to teach the stylists at the salon how to use the product. Woodyard has traveled all over the country during the past six years, while still keeping his full-time job, teaching color techniques at salons, and also participating in demonstrations for the company at trade shows. "I've taught all levels of classes," he says, "from a very basic color demonstration to a very complex color correction class. I've also been responsible for training other educators. I have really enjoyed traveling to other locales and having the opportunity to see other salons and other parts of the beauty and fashion industry."

Cosmetic Product Categories

- Baby products
- Bath preparations
- Eye makeup preparations
- Fragrance preparations
- Hair preparations (noncoloring)
- Hair coloring preparations
- Makeup preparations
- Manicuring preparations
- Oral hygiene products
- Personal cleanliness products
- Shaving preparations
- Skin care preparations
- Suntan preparations

Source: The Cosmetic, Toiletry, and Fragrance Association

At industry shows, what he does has varied. Woodyard is representing the company, whether he's standing behind a booth selling products or working on stage, demonstrating the product, or assisting a guest artist backstage, doing preparatory work. "This has given me a real hands-on education," he says, "and I've been able to work with some of the top hairstylists in the country."

Woodyard has been working, as he says, "behind the chair" for 14 years. His first job after graduating from cosmetology school was at a small barbershop in his hometown. From there, he moved on to a larger salon and then on to work in a big city. "Work behind the chair led me to want to do color," he said. "This really interested me. I guess wanting to know more about it myself is the reason why I researched it and became so involved with color. As I learned more about hair coloring, I became competent and more confident." The challenge, he said, is to learn the "laws of color"— how to choose a shade to get a specific result on a client's hair. He is now considered a color expert and is the head of the chemical department at his salon. "I've always been involved some way in outside education," Woodyard notes. "I've never been in a job where I have just worked 40 hours behind the chair. I've always been involved in some kind of training. I like to share what I know."

Cosmetologists must know how to market themselves to build their business. Whether they are self-employed or work for a salon or company, they are in business for themselves. It is the cosmetologist's skills and personality that will attract or fail to attract clients to that particular cosmetologist's chair. A marketing strategy Woodyard uses is to give several of his business cards to each of his clients. When one of his clients recommends him to a prospective new client, he gives both the old and new client a discount on a hair service.

Karol Thousand is the managing director of corporate school operations for a large cosmetology school that has four campuses in metropolitan areas in two states. She began as a stylist employed by salons and then owned her own shop for seven years. Her business was in an area that was destroyed by a tornado. It was then that she looked at different opportunities to decide the direction of her career. "I looked at the business end of the profession," she said, "and I took some additional business courses and was then introduced to the school aspect of the profession. I have a passion for the beauty business, and as I explored various training programs, I thought to myself, 'Hey, this is something I'd like to do!'"

She managed a cosmetology school in Wisconsin before moving to Chicago for her current position. "This is an empowering and satisfying profession," she says. "Not only do you make someone look better, but 99 percent of the time, they will feel better about themselves. In cosmetology, you can have the opportunity several times a day to help change the total look and perspective of an individual."

Cosmetologists serving the public must have pleasant, friendly, yet professional attitudes, as well as skill, ability, and an interest in their craft. These qualities are necessary in building a following of steady customers. The nature of their work requires cosmetologists to be aware of the psychological aspects of dealing with all types of personalities. Sometimes this can require diplomacy skills and a high degree of tolerance in dealing with different clients.

"To me," Sean Woodyard admits, "doing hair is just as much about self-gratification as it is about pleasing the client. It makes me feel good to make somebody else look good and feel good. It's also, of course, a great artistic and creative outlet."

REQUIREMENTS

High School

High school students interested in the cosmetology field can help build a good foundation for postsecondary training by taking subjects in the areas of art, science (especially a basic chemistry course), health, business, and communication arts. Psychology and speech courses could also be helpful.

Postsecondary Training

To become a licensed cosmetologist, you must have completed an undergraduate course of a certain amount of classroom credit hours. The required amount varies from state to state—anywhere from 1,050 to 2,200 hours. The program takes from 10 to 24 months to complete, again depending on the state. Evening courses are also frequently offered, and these take two to four months longer to complete. Applicants must also pass a written test, and some states also give an oral test, before they receive a license. Most states will allow a cosmetologist to work as an apprentice until the license is received, which normally just involves a matter of weeks.

A 1,500-hour undergraduate course at a cosmetology school in Illinois is typical of schools around the country. The program consists of theoretical and practical instruction divided into individual units of learning. Students are taught through the media of theory, audiovisual presentation, lectures, demonstrations, practical hands-on experiences, and written and practical testing. All schools have what they call clinic areas or floors, where people can have their hair done (or avail themselves of esthetics or nail services) by students at a discounted price, compared to what they would pay in a regular shop or salon.

One course, Scientific Approach to Hair Sculpture, teaches students how to sculpt straight and curly hair, ethnic and Caucasian, using shears, texturizing tools and techniques, razors, and electric clippers. Teaching tools include mannequins, slip-ons, hair wefts, rectangles, and profiles. People-skills segments are part of each course. Among other courses are Scientific Approach to Perm Design, Systematic Approach to Color, and Systematic Approach to Beauty Care. Three different salon prep courses focus on retailing, business survival skills, and practical applications for contemporary design. The program concludes with final testing, as well as extensive reviews and preparations for state board testing through a mock state board written practical examination.

Karol Thousand notes that at her school and others throughout the country, courses once focused mainly on technical skills. "This is still the core focus, but now we teach more interpersonal skills," she says. "Our people skills program helps students understand the individual, the different personality types—to better comprehend how they fit in and how to relate to their clients. We also teach sales and marketing skills—how to sell themselves and their services and products, as well as good business management skills."

Some states offer student internship programs. One such program that was recently initiated in Illinois aims to send better-prepared students/junior stylists into the workforce upon completion of their training from a licensed school. This program allows students to enter into a work-study program for 10 percent of their training in either cosmetology, esthetics, or nail technology. The state requires a student to complete at least 750 hours of training prior to making application for the program.

The program allows a student to experience firsthand the expectations of a salon, to perform salon services to be evaluated by their supervisor, and to experience different types of salon settings. The participating salons have the opportunity to prequalify potential employees before they graduate and work with the school regarding the skill levels of the student interns. This will also enhance job placement programs already in place in the school. The state requires that each participating salon be licensed and registered with the appropriate state department and file proof of registration with the school, along with the name and license number of their cosmetologist who is assigned to supervise students, before signing a contract or agreement.

Certification or Licensing

At the completion of the proper amount of credit hours, students must pass a formal examination before they can be licensed. The exam takes just a few hours. Some states also require a practical (hands-on) test and oral exams. Most, however, just require written tests. State board examinations are given at regular intervals. After about a month, test scores are available. Those who have passed then send in a licensure application and a specified fee to the appropriate state department. It takes about four to six weeks for a license to be issued.

Temporary permits are issued in most states, allowing students who have passed the test and applied for a license to practice their profession while they wait to receive the actual license.

Graduate courses on advanced techniques and new methods and styles are also available at many cosmetology schools. Many states require licensed cosmetologists to take a specified number of credit hours, called continuing education units, or CEUs.

In the majority of states, the minimum age for an individual to obtain a cosmetology license is 16. Because standards and requirements vary from state to state, students are urged to contact the licensing board of the state in which they plan to be employed.

Other Requirements

Hairstyles change from season to season. As a cosmetologist, you will need to keep up with current fashion trends and often be learning new procedures to create new looks. You should be able to visualize different styles and make suggestions to your clients about what is best for them. And even if you don't specialize in coloring hair, you should have a good sense of color. One of your most important responsibilities will be to make your clients feel comfortable around you and happy with their looks. To do this, you will need to develop both your talking and listening skills.

EXPLORING

Talk to friends or parents of friends who are working in the industry, or just go to a local salon or cosmetology school and ask questions about the profession. Go to the library and get books on careers in the beauty/hair care industry. Search the Internet for related Web sites. Individuals with an interest in the field might seek after-school or summer employment as a general shop helper in a barbershop or a salon. Some schools may permit potential students to visit and observe classes.

EMPLOYERS

Approximately 339,000 cosmetologists, hairdressers, and hairstylists are employed in the United States. The most common employers of hairstylists are, of course, beauty salons. However, hairstylists also find work at department stores, hospitals, nursing homes, spas, resorts, cruise ships, and cosmetics companies. The demand for services in the cosmetology field—hairstyling in particular—far exceeds the supply; additionally, the number of salons increases by 2 percent each year. Considering that most cosmetology schools have placement services to assist graduates, finding employment usually is not difficult for most cosmetologists. As with most jobs in the cosmetology field, opportunities will be concentrated in highly populated areas; however, there will be jobs available for hairstylists virtually everywhere. Many hairstylists/cosmetologists aspire ultimately to be self-employed. This can be a rewarding avenue if one has plenty of experience and good business sense (not to mention start-up capital or financial backing); it also requires long hours and a great deal of hard work.

STARTING OUT

To be a licensed cosmetologist/hairstylist, you must graduate from an accredited school and pass a state test. Once that is accomplished, you can apply for jobs that are advertised in the newspapers or over the Internet, or apply at an employment agency specializing in these professions. Most schools have placement services to help their graduates find jobs. Some salons have training programs from which they hire new employees.

Scholarships or grants that can help you pay for your schooling are available. One such program is the Access to Cosmetology Education (ACE) Grant. It is sponsored by the American Association of Cosmetology Schools (AACS) and the Cosmetology Advancement Foundation. Interested students can find out about ACE Grants and obtain applications at participating schools, salons, and distributors or through these institutions. The criteria for receiving an ACE Grant include approval from an AACS member school, recommendations from two salons, and a high school diploma or GED.

ADVANCEMENT

Individuals in the beauty/hair care industry most frequently begin by working at a shop or salon. Many aspire to be self-employed and own their own shop. There are many factors to consider when contemplating going into business on one's own. Usually it is essential to obtain experience and financial capital before seeking to own a shop. The cost of equipping even a one-chair shop can be very high. Owning a large shop or a chain of shops is an aspiration for the very ambitious.

Some pursue advanced educational training in one aspect of beauty culture, such as hairstyling or coloring. Others who are more interested in the business aspects can take courses in business management skills and move into shop or salon management, or work for a corporation related to the industry. Manufacturers and distributors frequently have exciting positions available for those with exceptional talent and creativity. Cosmetologists work on the stage as platform artists, or take some additional education courses and teach at a school of cosmetology.

Some schools publish their own texts and other printed materials for students. They want people who have cosmetology knowledge and experience as well as writing skills to write and edit these materials. An artistic director for the publishing venue of one large school has a cosmetology degree in addition to degrees in art. Other cosmetologists might design hairstyles for fashion magazines, industry publications, fashion shows, television presentations, or movies. They might get involved in the regulation of the business, such as working for a state licensing board. There are many and varied career possibilities cosmetologists can explore in the beauty/hair care industry.

EARNINGS

Cosmetologists can make an excellent living in the beauty/hair care industry, but as in most careers, they don't receive very high pay when just starting out. Though their raise in salary may start slowly, the curve quickly escalates. The U.S. Department of Labor reports cosmetologists and hairstylists had a median annual income (including tips) of $20,610 in 2005. The lowest paid 10 percent, which generally included those beginning in the profession, made less than $13,400. The highest paid 10 percent earned more than $37,380. Again, both those salaries include tips. On the extreme upper end of the pay scale, some fashion stylists in New York and Los Angeles charge $300 per haircut. Their annual salary can go into six figures. Salaries in larger cities are greater than those in smaller towns, but the cost of living is also higher in these cities.

Most shops and salons give a new employee a guaranteed income instead of commission. If the employee goes over the guaranteed amount, then he or she earns a commission. Usually, this guarantee will extend for the first three months of employment, so that the new stylist can focus on building up business before going on straight commission.

In addition, most salon owners grant incentives for product sales; and, of course, there are always tips. However, true professionals never depend on their tips. If a stylist receives a tip, it is a nice surprise for a job well done, but it is good business practice not to expect these bonuses. All tips must be recorded and reported to the Internal Revenue Service.

The benefits a cosmetologist receives, such as health insurance and retirement plans, depend on the place of employment. A small independent salon cannot afford to supply a hefty benefit package, but a large shop or salon or a member of a chain can be more generous. However, some of the professional associations and organizations offer benefit packages at reasonable rates.

WORK ENVIRONMENT

Those employed in the cosmetology industry usually work a five- or six-day week, which averages approximately 40 to 50 hours. Weekends and days preceding holidays may be especially busy. Cosmetologists are on their feet a lot and are usually working in a small space. Strict sanitation codes must be observed in all shops and salons, and they are comfortably heated, ventilated, and well-lighted.

Hazards of the trade include nicks and cuts from scissors and razors, minor burns when care is not used in handling hot towels or instruments, and occasional skin irritations arising from constant use of grooming aids that contain chemicals. Some of the chemicals used in hair dyes or permanent solutions can be very abrasive; plastic gloves are required for handling and contact. Pregnant women are advised to avoid contact with many of the chemicals present in hair products.

Conditions vary depending on what environment the stylist is working in. Those employed in department store salons will have more of a guaranteed client flow, with more walk-ins from people who are shopping. A freestanding shop or salon might have a more predictable pace, with more scheduled appointments and fewer walk-ins. In a department store salon, for example, stylists have to abide by the rules and regulations of the store. In a private salon, stylists are more like entrepreneurs or freelancers, but they have much more flexibility as to when they come and go and what type of business they want to do.

Stylist Sean Woodyard says, "I've always enjoyed the atmosphere of a salon. There's constant action and something different happening every day. A salon attracts artistic, creative people and the profession allows me to be part of the fashion industry."

Some may find it difficult to work constantly in such close, personal contact with the public at large, especially when they strive to satisfy customers who are difficult to please or disagreeable. The work demands an even temperament, pleasant disposition, and patience.

OUTLOOK

The future looks good for cosmetology. According to the U.S. Department of Labor, employment should grow about as fast as the average for all occupations through 2014. Our growing population, the availability of disposable income, and changes in hair fashion that are practically seasonal all contribute to the demand for cosmetologists. In addition, turnover in this career is fairly high as cosmetologists move up into management positions, change careers, or leave the field for other reasons. Competition for jobs at higher paying, prestigious salons, however, is strong.

FOR MORE INFORMATION

For information on cosmetology careers, schools, and the ACE Grant, contact

American Association of Cosmetology Schools
15825 North 71st Street, Suite 100
Scottsdale, AZ 85254-1521

Tel: 800-831-1086
http://www.beautyschools.org

To read Career Opportunities in the Cosmetic, Toiletry, and Fragrance Industry, *visit the following Web site*:
  The Cosmetic, Toiletry, and Fragrance Association
  1101 17th Street, NW, Suite 300
  Washington, DC 20036-4702
  Tel: 202-331-1770
  http://www.ctfa.org

For information on membership, contact
  Cosmetologists of America
  PO Box 1083
  Newport, RI 02840-0999
  Tel: 401-662-2181
  http://www.cosmetologistsofamerica.com

For information on accredited cosmetology programs, contact
  **National Accrediting Commission of Cosmetology Arts and
    Sciences**
  4401 Ford Avenue, Suite 1300
  Alexandria, VA 22302-1432
  Tel: 703-600-7600
  http://www.naccas.org

For information on scholarships, contact
  National Cosmetology Association
  401 North Michigan Avenue, 22nd Floor
  Chicago, IL 60611-4245
  Tel: 312-527-6765
  http://www.ncacares.org

Dermatologists

OVERVIEW

Dermatologists study, diagnose, and treat diseases and ailments of the skin, hair, mucous membranes, nails, and related tissues or structures. They may also perform cosmetic services, such as scar removal or hair transplants. There are approximately 567,000 physicians and surgeons of all types working in the United States. According to the American Medical Association, approximately 1.2 percent specialize in dermatology.

HISTORY

Many in the medical profession opposed specialization when it began to occur in the 19th century. They thought treatments would be too fragmented for patients' own good. There were several factors, however, that made specialization inevitable. The amount of medical information was increasing and complex new techniques were developing at such a rapid pace that doctors could not keep up with the advances. They began to send patients to physicians who concentrated on one type of illness or manipulation. Specialization was also attractive because it gave doctors the opportunity to demand higher fees, work fewer hours, and command greater respect from peers and the public. Medical experts gradually abandoned their ideas that general disease was caused by problems of the humors, or elemental fluids of the body, and began to diagnose and treat local organs instead.

The specialty of dermatology had its beginnings in the mid-1800s in Vienna when a doctor named Ferdinand von Hebra, one of the first to specialize entirely in skin diseases, founded a division of dermatology. At that time, medicine concentrated primarily on abnormalities in the four humors—blood, phlegm, black bile, and yellow bile—and they believed symptoms were caused by those abnormalities. Hebra made classifications based on changes in the tissues instead of on symptoms or on general disease categories. As a result, his treatment was directed toward the local problem rather than treating imbalances in the humors. He was responsible for the discovery that scabies was transmissible from person to person and could be cured by the destruction of the itch-mite parasite.

Innumerable discoveries have been made in the field of dermatology, including new medicines, treatments, and equipment. Lasers and computer technology, for example, have drastically changed dermatology, improving diagnostic techniques and allowing certain surgical procedures to be performed without using a scalpel.

THE JOB

Dermatologists study, diagnose, and treat diseases and ailments of the largest, most visible organ of the body, the skin, and its related tissues and structures: hair, mucous membranes, and nails. Their work begins with diagnosis to determine the cause of the disease or condition. This process involves studying a patient's history, conducting visual examinations, and taking blood samples, smears of the affected skin, microscopic scrapings, or biopsy specimens of the skin. They may order cultures of fungi or bacteria, or perform patch and photosensitivity tests to reveal allergies and immunologic diseases. They may also evaluate bone marrow, lymph nodes, and endocrine glands. Usually dermatologists send skin, tissue, or blood specimens to a laboratory for chemical and biological testing and analysis.

Dermatologists treat some skin problems with prescribed oral medications, such as antibiotics, or topical applications. Certain types of eczema and dermatitis, psoriasis, acne, or impetigo can usually be treated with creams, ointments, or oral medicines.

Exposure to ultraviolet light is used to treat such conditions as psoriasis, and radiation therapy is occasionally used to treat keloids (scar tissue that grows excessively).

Some skin conditions and illnesses require surgical treatment. There are three types of skin cancer—basal cell carcinoma, squamous cell carcinoma, and malignant melanoma—which must be removed surgically. Dermatologists may use traditional surgery, where the cancerous cells and surrounding tissue are cut away, but some cancers can be removed by lasers, frozen by cryosurgery, destroyed with a cautery device (high-frequency electric current), or destroyed by radiation therapy. Another type of surgery dermatologists use is Moh's surgery, in which progressive layers of skin and tissue are cut out and examined microscopically for the presence of cancers. Dermatologists also perform skin graft procedures to repair wounds that are too large to be stitched together. After removal of a skin tumor, for example, they take a portion of skin from another part of the patient's body, such as the thigh, and attach it to the wound. Since the skin graft comes from the patient's own body, there is no problem with rejection.

Not all surgeries that dermatologists perform are major. There are many conditions that can be treated with simple outpatient procedures under local anesthetic, including removal of warts, sebaceous cysts, scars, moles, cosmetic defects of the skin, boils, and abscesses. Hair transplants are usually done in the doctor's office, as are laser treatments for disfiguring birth defects, cysts, birthmarks, spider veins, and growths.

Certain diseases can manifest themselves in a skin condition. When dermatologists see that a skin problem is a sign of an illness in another part of the patient's body, they recommend treatment by other specialists. If a patient complains of itchy or scaly skin, for example, it may be an allergy. Boils may be a sign of diabetes mellitus, and a skin rash may indicate secondary syphilis. Dermatologists must often consult with allergists, internists, and other doctors. In turn, many dermatologists are called on by other specialists to help diagnose complicated symptoms.

Dermatologists not only deal with the physical aspects of skin afflictions, but the emotional aspects, too. Patients often have to face embarrassment, ridicule, and rejection because of their skin ailments, and dermatologists can help them overcome this kind of trauma.

Within the field of dermatology there are some subspecialties. *Dermatoimmunologists* focus on the treatment of diseases that involve the immune system, including allergies. They may use a procedure called immunofluorescence to diagnose and characterize these skin disorders. *Dermatopathologists* study the tissue structure and features of skin diseases. *Dermatologic surgeons* perform Moh's micrographic surgery and cosmetic procedures, including collagen injections, sclerotherapy (the injection of varicose veins with a fluid), and dermabrasion (a planing of the skin using sandpaper, wire brushes, or other abrasive materials). *Pediatric dermatologists* treat skin disorders in children. *Occupational dermatologists* study and treat occupational disorders, such as forms of dermatitis from chemical or biological irritants.

Some dermatologists combine a private practice with a teaching position at a medical school. Others are involved in research, developing new treatments, and finding cures for skin ailments. A few work in industry, developing cosmetics, lotions, and other consumer products.

REQUIREMENTS

High School

Dermatologists, like all physicians, have completed a great deal of education. You should realize that after high school your education will continue on through college, medical school, and a residency in your specialty. In high school you can start preparing for both college and your medical studies by taking science classes such as biology, chemistry, physics, and anatomy. Mathematics classes, such as algebra and geometry, will give you experience in working with numbers and formulas, both important skills for this career. Make sure your high school education is well-rounded and college preparatory by taking English and history classes as well as a foreign language. Also, psychology classes and other social science classes may give you a background in understanding people—an important skill for any doctor. Take this time to develop your study habits and determine how well you like the course of study.

Postsecondary Training

Your next step after high school is to earn a bachelor's degree, typically with a major in a science field such as biology or chemistry, from an accredited four-year college. Some schools may offer well-defined premedical courses of study, while others will allow you to structure your own education. In either case, your college studies should concentrate on the sciences, including biology, physics, organic chemistry, and inorganic chemistry. In addition, you should continue to take mathematics, English, and social science courses. Language classes, particularly Latin, may help you in your medical school studies.

While you are in your second or third year of college, you should arrange with an adviser to take the Medical College Admission Test (MCAT). All medical colleges in this country require this test for admission. After you receive your undergraduate degree, you can apply to one of the 148 medical schools in the United States. The admissions process is very competitive and includes evaluation by a committee that considers grade point averages, MCAT scores, and recommendations from professors. Most premedical students apply to several medical schools long before graduation, and only about one-third of all applicants are accepted. Medical school study and training lasts four years, at the end of which you will earn the degree of doctor of medicine (M.D.) or doctor of osteopathy (D.O.), the latter for those who attend an osteopathic medical school.

For the first two years of medical school, you will attend lectures and classes and spend time in laboratories. Courses include anatomy, biochemistry, physiology, pharmacology, psychology, microbiology, pathology, medical ethics, and laws governing medicine. Medical students learn to take patient histories, perform examinations, and recognize symptoms. In their third and fourth years, medical students are involved in more practical studies. They work in clinics and hospitals supervised by physicians learning acute, chronic, preventive, and rehabilitative care. They go through rotations in internal medicine, family practice, obstetrics and gynecology, pediatrics, psychiatry, and surgery in which they practice and learn the skills of diagnosing and treating illnesses.

After medical school, all physicians must pass an examination given by the National Board of Medical Examiners in order to receive a license from the state in which they intend to practice. Most physicians then begin their residency to learn a specialty. Only about half of the applicants for the accredited residency programs in the United States are accepted, and dermatology is very competitive.

Residency training for dermatologists lasts a minimum of four years, three of which are spent specializing in dermatology. The first year is a clinical residency program in internal medicine, family practice, general surgery, or pediatrics. The next three years are spent studying and practicing dermatology. Residents are closely supervised as they study skin pathology, bacteriology, radiology, surgery, biochemistry, allergy and immunology, and other basics. Intensive laboratory work in mycology (the study of the fungi that infect humans) is usually required. Following the residency, dermatologists can become certified by the American Board of Dermatology and have full professional standing.

Certification or Licensing

Certification in dermatology, as mentioned above, is given by the American Board of Dermatology. Although certification is voluntary, it is strongly recommended. Certification demonstrates the physician's dedication to the field, assures patients of his or her educational qualifications, and affirms that the physician has met the American Board of Dermatology's standards to practice this specialty. To qualify for certification, you must have completed your residency and pass written and sometimes practical examinations given by the American Board of Dermatology. Certification is for a period of 10 years. Even after 11 years of study, dermatologists must continue to study throughout their careers in order to keep up with medical advances and retain board certification.

All physicians in the United States must be licensed to practice. Some states have reciprocity agreements with other states so that a physician licensed in one state may be automatically licensed in another without being required to pass another examination.

Other Requirements
Medical school and the dermatological residency are filled with stress and pressure, and they are also physically demanding. Residents often work 30-hour shifts and put in as many as 80 hours a week. They need to be emotionally stable in order to handle the stress of this intense schedule. Physicians need self-confidence because they make decisions on critical medical issues. They must also have keen observation skills, be detail oriented, and have excellent memories. Finally, because this is a people job, physicians need to be able to relate to people with compassion and understanding.

EXPLORING

You may be able to schedule a time at a dermatologist's office for a tour of the facilities. When making the appointment, explain that you are interested in a dermatology career and ask if you could set up an informational interview with the doctor. Go to the interview prepared with questions about topics that concern you. What, for example, was the most difficult aspect of the schooling? What are the most rewarding aspects of the work? What advice would the doctor give to someone interested in pursuing this career?

If you are unable to visit a dermatologist's office, try to tour other medical settings such as hospitals, clinics, and health care facilities. Talk to your family doctor about the field of medicine in general and explain your interest. Your family doctor may have contacts who would be happy to speak to you if they know of your plans.

You should certainly try to do volunteer work in a hospital, clinic, or even nursing home. Volunteer work will give you exposure to a health care environment, practical experience, and allow you to gauge how well you like working in the medical field. In addition, such experience will add to your credentials when you apply to college and medical school.

EMPLOYERS

Most dermatologists are in private practice, either individually or with others. A few work for hospitals or similar health agencies. Some establish their practices at large university medical centers in order to combine an active practice with teaching at a university or medical school. Researchers work in university or private laboratories searching for new cures and treatments.

STARTING OUT

Once a doctor finishes the residency program, there are several options for beginning to practice dermatology. The most difficult is to set up a private practice. It is a considerable expense to purchase the necessary equipment and supplies, pay staff salaries, rent office space, pay liability insurance, and advertise. It can take up to 15 years to become established and reach full earning potential.

A second option is to take over the practice of a dermatologist who is retiring or relocating. This has the benefit of offering an already existing patient list.

Some dermatologists join a group practice or enter into partnership with a related medical specialist such as an allergist, an immunologist, or a plastic surgeon.

Many newly qualified dermatologists are much more likely to take salaried jobs in group medical practices, clinics, or health maintenance organizations. After several years, they may decide to open their own practice. Some find opportunities with federal or state agencies, private businesses, or the military.

ADVANCEMENT

Dermatologists with their own private practices can increase their earnings or improve their clinical status by expanding their practices or moving to larger cities. They may become teachers at medical schools in addition to treating patients, or they may go into research.

Some go into hospital administration, where they have less contact with patients and more involvement with staff and the day-to-day operation of the hospital.

Many physicians participate in national organizations, such as the American Medical Association or the American Academy of Dermatology, where they can serve on committees and be elected to offices, increasing their status.

EARNINGS

Earnings for dermatologists are affected by number of years in practice, geographic region, hours worked, and the skill, personality, and professional standing of the doctor. According to *Physicians Compensation Survey,* published by the recruiting agency Physicians Search, dermatologists in their first year of practice earned an average salary of $160,000 in 2007, and salaries ranged from $120,000 to $225,000. Dermatologists who had been practicing for three years earned an average of $232,000. Their salaries ranged from $168,988 to $407,000.

Dermatologists in private practice or group partnerships have the potential for higher earnings, but they must cover all of their own business expenses and benefits. Dermatologists hired by health care organizations may receive benefits, including health and life insurance, malpractice liability insurance, paid vacation, and retirement plans, in addition to salary. Some earn productivity bonuses as well.

WORK ENVIRONMENT

Dermatologists are often solo practitioners. They work in well-lighted, air-conditioned offices, and they are usually assisted by clerical and nursing staff. A certain number of hours are spent each week visiting patients at the hospital. Most dermatologists also spend some time in laboratory settings, either their own or in a hospital. Most specialists, including dermatologists, work in large urban areas.

Working hours are usually regular, since dermatologists see patients by appointment in their offices. They schedule surgeries and follow-up visits both at their offices and at hospitals. Dermatologists occasionally may have to answer emergency calls, such as to treat burn victims.

Dermatologists work 40 to 50 hours a week, mostly during normal daytime hours, though some work up to 60 hours a week. They often try to accommodate the working schedules of their patients by opening their offices on Saturdays or one evening a week.

OUTLOOK

The health care industry is thriving, and the U.S. Department of Labor predicts that employment for physicians will grow faster than the average for all occupations through 2014. The field of dermatology is expected to expand for a number of reasons. New technologies, medicines, and treatments continue to be developed at a rapid pace. Another factor in the growth of this industry is that the average age of the American population is rising, and older people require more skin-related health care. Demand for dermatologists has increased as people have become aware of the effects of radiation exposure from the sun and of air pollutants on skin. The public is also much more aware of the benefits of good general and dermatological health.

FOR MORE INFORMATION

The AAD can provide good medical information on dermatological conditions as well as employment opportunities and professional concerns. Kids' Connection on its Web site provides information on dermatology for children age eight through adolescence.
American Academy of Dermatology (AAD)
PO Box 4014
Schaumburg, IL 60618-4014
Tel: 866-503-7546
Email: mrc@aad.org
http://www.aad.org

For information on certification and other career materials, contact
American Board of Dermatology
Henry Ford Health System
One Ford Place
Detroit, MI 48202-3450
Tel: 313-874-1088
Email: abderm@hfhs.org
http://www.abderm.org

For more information on the medical profession in general and about certain medical conditions, check out the following Web site:
American Medical Association
515 North State Street
Chicago, IL 60610-5453
Tel: 800-621-8335
http://www.ama-assn.org

Electrologists

OVERVIEW

Electrologists are trained professionals who remove hair from the skin of patients. The electrologist uses a probe to shoot an electric wave into the papilla, or root, of the hair to kill the root and deter new hair growth. Since the root may not be destroyed on the first try, it is often necessary to treat the same area many times over a period of months or even years.

HISTORY

Since many people today find excess facial or body hair unattractive, numerous convenient and affordable methods of hair removal are available. Depilatories are sometimes used to dissolve the hair, but they have the potential to irritate the skin and often have unpleasant odors. Shaving, or cutting the hair close to the skin with a blade or razor (one of the most popular methods of controlling body hair) can lead to skin cuts, chafing, and ingrown hairs. With waxing, a warm wax is applied to the area where hair is to be removed. A piece of cloth is then placed on the wax and ripped off quickly, ripping out the attached hairs. Sugaring is based on the same principle but is said to be safer since it uses a cool solution instead of hot wax. Both sugaring and waxing can lead to increased skin sensitivity and ingrown hairs. With tweezing, the hairs are plucked individually with small forceps. This is usually more effective for small, delicate areas of the body, such as the eyebrow area, where other hair removal techniques might be dangerous or less effective. Shaving, sugaring, waxing, and tweezing have all been used to provide temporary solutions for hairiness, but

School Subjects
Anatomy
Biology
Health

Personal Skills
Helping/teaching
Mechanical/manipulative

Work Environment
Primarily indoors
Primarily one location

Minimum Education Level
Some postsecondary training

Salary Range
$15,970 to $25,000 to $50,000

Certification or Licensing
Voluntary (certification)
Required by certain states (licensing)

Outlook
About as fast as the average

DOT
N/A

GOE
11.04.01

NOC
6482

O*NET-SOC
N/A

these methods only cut or temporarily remove the hair; they do nothing to prevent future growth. Electrolysis is the only method reported to remove unwanted hair permanently, and when performed by a professional electrologist, it can be safer than many chemical products and other treatments.

The practice of electrology began in 1869, when Dr. Charles E. Michel, a Missouri ophthalmologist, used a probe and electric current to remove ingrown eyelashes for his patients. In the early 1900s, the multiple-needle technique for galvanic electrolysis was developed. Around the same time, Dr. Henri Bordier, of Lyon, France, developed the method of thermolysis, or electrolysis, using short waves and a high frequency. Improvements throughout the years have led to safer treatments. A current trend in electrology is the development and use of computerized equipment that delivers a safer and more reliable electrical charge. Disposable needles and other materials are also becoming the norm. Improvements in equipment and more stringent standardization procedures for certification of machinery and operators are making electrolysis safer and more accessible to all.

THE JOB

Electrologists, who usually conduct business in a professional office, salon, or medical clinic, work with only one patron at a time. This enables them to focus their complete attention and concentration on the delicate treatment they are performing. Since electrolysis can sometimes be uncomfortable, it reassures patrons to know that the practitioner's complete focus is on them and their needs. A high level of professionalism helps patients put their trust in the electrologist and may make them more receptive to the treatment.

Electrologists often begin their work with a personal consultation. It is essential for electrologists to interview potential clients to understand why they want to have the hair removed and what expectations they have about the procedure. The electrologist should explain the process in detail, discussing possible side effects as well as the effectiveness and duration of individual sessions and approximate length of time before the treatments are complete. A good electrologist also may suggest alternate methods of hair removal that may be more cost effective or appropriate for different clients and their needs.

Before beginning a session, the electrologist needs to make sure that the areas to be treated and all instruments used are sterile. A sanitary work environment is crucial for the safety of the electrologist as well as the person undergoing treatment. The electrologist may have an assistant or trainee help with these preparations. The first step in the treatment session is the cleansing of the area of skin that will be treated. Rubbing alcohol or an antiseptic is often used for this purpose. Once the skin is cleansed, hair removal can begin. Electrologists use a round-tipped probe to enter the opening of the skin fold, also known as the hair follicle. The probe also penetrates the papilla, which is the organ beneath the hair root. The electrologist sets the proper amount and duration of the electrical current in advance and presses gently on a floor pedal to distribute that current through the probe. The electrical current helps deaden the tissue, after which the hair can be lifted out gently with a pair of tweezers or forceps.

Electrologists determine the extent of treatments that will be necessary for complete removal of the unwanted hair. They may schedule weekly appointments that last 15, 30, 45, or even 60 minutes. The length of the individual appointments depends on both the amount of hair to be removed and the thickness and depth of the hair. Very coarse hair may take longer to treat, whereas fine hair may be permanently removed in only a few sessions. If a patient is very sensitive to the treatments, the electrologist may set up shorter appointments or schedule more time between sessions. Some electrologists use a gold needle on sensitive clients to minimize adverse reactions, which can include itching, bumps, redness, and pustules. Most of these reactions can be treated with topical ointments and proper skin care.

Electrologists can remove hair from almost any area of the body. The most common areas they treat are the arms, legs, chest, and portions of the face such as upper or lower lip, chin, or cheek. Electrologists should not remove hair from inside the ears or nose or from the eyelids. They should also have the written consent of a physician to remove hair from a mole or birthmark. As with many professions, electrologists should have legitimate malpractice insurance coverage.

As with all cosmetic treatments, the procedure can be fairly expensive. Since electrolysis is performed mainly for aesthetic reasons, it is generally not covered by any health insurance plans. Also, electrolysis is not a quick fix. Constant maintenance is necessary for some clients, and people often have electrolysis treatments for years in certain areas before the hair root is finally destroyed.

REQUIREMENTS

High School

While you are in high school you should take classes in science, anatomy, physiology, and health if you are interested in pursuing a career as an electrologist. These classes will give you a good understanding of the human body and its functions. Learning about hair and how it grows, in addition to the theories and practices of electrology, can help a potential electrologist decide if this is the proper career path for him or her. In addition, you should consider taking classes in communications, psychology, and bookkeeping, accounting, or business management. These classes will give you skills for working well with people as well as help you if you decide to establish your own practice.

Postsecondary Training

Once you have gotten your high school diploma or equivalency certificate, you can enroll in a trade school or professional school that offers electrolysis training. The quality of these programs may vary, so you should look for programs that offer courses of study in such areas as microbiology, dermatology, neurology, and electricity. You will also learn about proper sterilization and sanitation procedures to avoid infections or injury to yourself or your clients. Classes that cover cell composition, the endocrine system, the vascular pulmonary system, and basic anatomy will also be beneficial to you.

Although the training offered is designed to educate students about the theory of electrolysis and its relation to the skin and tissue, the greater part of the training is of a practical nature. You will spend many training hours learning the purpose and function of the different types of equipment. In addition, hands-on experience with patrons needing different treatments will give you confidence in operating equipment and working with people.

Programs may be offered on a full-time or part-time basis. Although tuition varies, some schools offer financial assistance or payment plans to make their programs more affordable. Sometimes lab and materials fees are charged. Check if the school you are interested in is accredited or associated with any professional organizations. Also, consider what state you want to work in after graduation. Licensing requirements of the various states may affect the length and type of training that the schools offer.

Certification or Licensing

Certification, while voluntary, can indicate your commitment to the profession. A number of certification options are available. For example, the designation of certified professional electrologist (CPE) is offered by the American Electrology Association through the International Board of Electrologist Certification. The Society for Clinical and Medical Hair Removal offers three certification levels through its International Commission for Hair Removal Certification: certified clinical electrologist, certified medical electrologist, and certified laser hair removal professional.

Thirty-four states require electrologists to be licensed. Those with this requirement offer the licensing examinations through their state health departments or boards of barbering cosmetology. The examination usually covers various topics in the areas of health and cosmetology. Most states require applicants for electrology licensing to have a minimum number of study hours and practical training. They must also pass a written theory examination, a state exam, and a clinical examination. You should become familiar with your state's licensing requirements prior to beginning your training so you can be sure your education provides you with everything necessary to practice.

Other Requirements

Electrologists help people feel good about themselves by improving aspects of their physical appearance. People with excess body hair see the procedure as a way for them to have a "normal" life, in which they do not have to rely on temporary methods to remove hair or hide hairy areas. Electrologists feel a great sense of accomplishment through helping people with the various stages of their treatment and helping them to achieve their hair removal goals. They may sometimes feel the anxiety of a client who is impatient or unrealistic about the results or is nervous about the process. Because electrologists perform personal and sometimes uncomfortable treatments, it is important that they be patient and caring and develop an empathetic working style. A potential electrologist also should not be squeamish, since the procedure involves probes. Since the area to be treated is sometimes delicate, electrologists need to have good visual acuity and coordination to perform the procedures, although special accommodations may be made for practitioners with different abilities.

EXPLORING

To find out more about the field of electrology, try contacting local trade schools for information. Also, some two-year colleges that offer course work in medical technician careers may be able to supply you with literature on programs and training in electrology. If you are particularly interested in the field, make an appointment for an electrolysis consultation and perhaps pursue treatment for yourself.

Cosmetology schools, which are located in many different areas of the country, may also prove helpful for investigating this profession. Most schools and training programs allow interested students to speak with faculty and guidance counselors for further information. Ask if you can sit in on classes or contact a certified electrologist or patient of electrology to find out more about the field and procedures.

EMPLOYERS

Electrologists are employed by salons, professional offices, and medical clinics, or they may be self-employed. In some cases, experienced electrologists may hire newly licensed electrologists as assistants.

STARTING OUT

Many electrologists begin as assistants to a practicing professional. These assistants may handle extra patients when the office is overbooked or have new patients referred to them. In this way, beginning electrologists can build a clientele without having to cover the high costs of equipment, supplies, and office space. Often, trade schools have job placement offices that help new electrologists build a practice. Also, some schools may offer alumni mentor programs, through which the school introduces a new graduate to an established electrologist for mutual benefit. The new graduate can introduce new theories and practices to the professional and take care of overflow clients, while the established professional can help the new electrologist build a client base and start his or her own practice.

Some electrologists may choose to open their own business in a medical office complex and receive referrals from their neighboring health care professionals. Clinics or hospitals may also employ electrologists before they get their own office space. Beauty salons and health spas may have an electrologist on staff who can provide initial consultations with clients considering different methods of hair removal.

ADVANCEMENT

As an electrologist becomes more experienced and gains a reputation, he or she often attracts more new patrons and repeat clients. Some electrologists who work as part of a clinic staff may open their own office in a more visible or accessible location.

By obtaining additional training and education, electrologists can often branch out into other fields, including cosmetology and medicine. An electrologist trained in other methods may decide to offer clients additional hair removal procedures, such as waxing, sugaring, or laser hair removal. Electrologists can also become certified to teach the theory and practice of electrology in trade schools. Electrologists may also use their writing skills and practical experience to contribute to trade magazines, journals, and Web sites devoted to the field.

EARNINGS

Because electrologists schedule client treatments that vary in length, their fees are often based on quarter-hour appointments. Rates for a 15-minute treatment may begin at $15 in some cities, while charges in large urban regions may begin at $30. Treatments lasting 30 or 60 minutes in large cities may begin at $50 and $100, respectively. Although rates in smaller towns are often lower, electrologists there still earn a competitive wage for their work.

Salary.com reports that electrologists earned a median salary of approximately $20,000 in 2007, with the lowest 25 percent earning less than $15,970, and the highest 25 percent earning more than $23,939. The American Electrology Association reports that full-time, established electrologists can earn between $25,000 and $50,000 per year. Electrologists who are employed by a medical clinic or salon may have to contribute a portion of their fees to help cover office space, utilities, and support staff such as receptionists and bookkeepers.

Electrologists employed by a salon or group practice generally get the same benefits as other employees, which may include health, dental, and life insurance, as well as disability coverage, retirement savings plans, and paid vacations. Self-employed electrologists usually must provide these things for themselves.

WORK ENVIRONMENT

Whether the electrologist works in a professional office, a salon, a medical clinic, or a private shop, the nature of the work requires the environment to be clean, comfortable, and professional. Because electrologists perform delicate work, they may operate in spaces that are quiet to allow for greater concentration for the practitioner and to relax the client. Sometimes soothing music is played in the background to help put clients at ease.

A neat and professional appearance is important, so electrologists often wear uniforms or lab coats. As well as being comfortable and practical for the electrologist, a medical uniform may also reassure and comfort the client. Because of the threat of infectious diseases, electrologists may wear eye protection and disposable gloves during the procedure to reduce their risk of exposure. They also wash their hands frequently and maintain a sterile treatment area.

Electrologists generally spend most of their time in an office or treatment room, although not all that time is spent with clients. When not working on clients, electrologists may set up appointments, consult with prospective clients, train an assistant or future electrologist, or check equipment to ensure that it is functioning properly.

OUTLOOK

The U.S. Department of Labor predicts that employment for those in the cosmetology field, which includes electrologists, will increase about as fast as average for all occupations through 2014. Many salons, professional offices, and hospitals and clinics are striving to offer cutting-edge technologies and services to maintain—or gain—a competitive edge, which will create more jobs for electrologists. Further, the demand for electrologists is growing due to the increased awareness of and interest in this service. There are generally greater opportunities for electrologists in larger cities and highly populated areas.

Since electrology has been in practice for over a century, many clients are feeling more comfortable with the procedure. Also, with more disposable income, people who once considered permanent hair removal a luxury are beginning to consider electrolysis an affordable option.

FOR MORE INFORMATION

For information regarding the International Board of Electrologist Certification, careers, and for a directory of accredited schools and specific state requirements relating to electrology, contact
American Electrology Association
Public Information Committee
PO Box 687
Bodega Bay, CA 94923-0687
Tel: 707-875-9135
Email: careeraea@electrology.com
http://www.electrology.com

For career, certification, and continuing education information, contact
Society for Clinical and Medical Hair Removal
2810 Crossroads Drive, Suite 3800
Madison, WI 53718-7961

Tel: 608-443-2470
Email: homeoffice@scmhr.org
http://www.scmhr.org

━━━━━ INTERVIEW ━━━━━

Joyce Munson has been an electrologist since 1988 and is the owner of the Eau Claire Institute of Electrology in Eau Claire, Wisconsin. She discussed her career with the editors of Careers in Focus: Cosmetology.

Q. Please tell us about your background and school.

A. My original career was that of a registered nurse, after graduating from the University of Wisconsin–Eau Claire with a bachelor of science in nursing. I worked in the nursing field for more than 11 years before I received my electrology training through the Electrolysis Research Institute School of Electrolysis. After practicing as an electrologist in a dermatology clinic, and later my own electrolysis establishment, I went on to become a licensed electrology instructor, and now own my own state-licensed school of electrology.

Typically the only educational prerequisite to taking an electrology course is a high school diploma or GED, but this varies from state to state. Not all states require licensure or regulate the profession. Currently 34 states regulate the practice of electrology, and most electrologists are licensed through state boards of barbering cosmetology or state departments of health. Typical hours of training are 450 hours to 600 hours, again varying from state to state. Regardless of state mandates, I would highly encourage attending a licensed educational program to assure a quality education to prepare you to meet the challenges of this career, and to practice safely and successfully. Becoming nationally certified is a further step in achieving recognition of your knowledge base and proof of continuing education.

Our school, Eau Claire Institute of Electrology, was founded in 1994. As a Wisconsin state-licensed school, it offers training to individuals from any state, with its curriculum tailored to meet each state's guidelines. Wisconsin mandates a 450-hour specified course of training, typically over 13 and a half weeks. Our very complete curriculum includes theoretical and practical hands-on training in all three modalities: thermolysis (flash and manual), galvanic (including multiple needle), and the blend, as well as phoresis. We also include training in entrepreneurship, safety and sanitation, and law and code. Our school is unique, in that it combines a thriving electrology establishment in conjunction with the school, allowing the student to be integrated into a real, operating business while learning and practicing their skills.

Q. Why did you decide to become an electrologist?

A. After successfully working over 11 years in hospital and home care settings, I sought a job that would allow me to better meet my family's needs and schedules. It was difficult to work a nursing job that demanded swing shifts, call schedules, holidays, and weekends, and still feel that I was doing a good job as mother and wife. It was while I was working for a dermatologist that I saw the need for an electrologist in this area, so I obtained the education. Before long, I realized that working independently as an electrologist offered many benefits, so I pursued that direction.

Q. Take us through a day in your life as an electrologist. What are your typical tasks/responsibilities?

A. A typical day in my work schedule as an electrologist would be going into my office and treating eight to 10 clients. I commonly spend between 15 and 60 minutes with each client doing the process of hair removal, assessing their progress, and modifying the treatment approach to obtain the best results. Ongoing education of the client throughout the process aids them in adhering to their treatment schedule, as a client typically requires 12 to 18 months of treatment to achieve permanent results. As the owner of a small business, I also share with my employees the duties of secretary, receptionist, and housekeeper. I am the employer, the bookkeeper, and the person in charge of making sure everything runs smoothly. I make sure we have an inventory of supplies readily available, meet with advertising media reps, and promote our business through speaking engagements and community involvement.

Membership in professional groups is also a vital part of being a business owner. I am a member of our chamber of commerce, the Wisconsin Electrologists' Association, and the American Electrology Association. Attending conferences for ongoing learning has given me the opportunity to travel throughout our state and nation and has opened up networking opportunities for my personal and professional growth.

Q. What do you like most and least about your job?

A. What I like the most about my job is the contact with people, and helping them to feel better about themselves. This job is extremely rewarding from a personal perspective. I have seen how electrolysis can transform an individual's self-esteem and make a positive impact on their life.

The other big advantages of this career are the ability to have some flexibility in my work hours, and the opportunity to obtain a lucrative salary that is reflective of the degree of work I put into my job. Though one must keep in mind the availability of the clients in establishing a work schedule, having the flexibility of working around my family's schedule and needs has been wonderful. In this career, an individual can be an employee, own their own business as a sole practitioner, or have employees. Operating your own business can be exhilarating, challenging, and rewarding. Electrology is a small field in which you can grow to whatever size or level you choose, from an employee to owner of a full-service salon or spa, from a local level, to an expanded national level.

As for what I like least, it is probably similar to what you would find in any career. If you are self-employed, the benefits of insurance and pension are not provided to you, but must be purchased, and all of the liability and risk of running a business falls on your shoulders. If you are an employee, you are required to meet the expectations of your employer and work within their framework.

Q. What advice would you give to high school students who are interested in this career?

A. Take advantage of any opportunity that would allow you to work with the public. Care-giving opportunities in the health care profession, such as certified nursing assistant work, can help prepare you for working closely with people and developing an empathy for dealing with potentially embarrassing problems. Working in a small business setting can help you develop business savvy and experience in dealing with the public and office protocol. If you think that you will want to own your own business some day, joining a club such as Junior Achievement or participating in leadership roles through student council, 4-H, or school-related groups may be extremely helpful. Seek out an opportunity to visit or shadow a person in the profession. Learn how to do a feasibility study to see if there is a need for an electrologist in the community you would like to practice. You may want to contact the U.S. Small Business Administration to further assist you if you plan on starting your own business.

Makeup Artists

OVERVIEW

Makeup artists prepare actors for performances on stage and before cameras. They read scripts and consult with directors, producers, and technicians to design makeup effects for each individual character. They apply makeup and prosthetics and build and style wigs. They also create special makeup effects. Approximately 2,000 makeup artists are employed in the United States.

HISTORY

Theatrical makeup is as old as the theater itself. Cultures around the world performed ritualistic dances, designed by spiritual leaders, to communicate with gods and other supernatural forces. These dances often involved elaborate costumes and makeup. By the Elizabethan age, theater had become an entertainment requiring special makeup techniques to transform the male actors into female characters. In Asia in the 17th century, Kabuki theater maintained the symbolic origins of the drama; actors wore very stylized makeup to depict each character's nature and social standing. It was not until the late 18th century in Europe that plays, and therefore costumes and makeup, were based on realistic portrayals of society. The grease stick, a special makeup stick that could withstand harsh stage lights without smearing, was invented in the 19th century.

This grease stick led the way for other advancements in the chemistry of stage makeup, but even today's makeup artists must use ingenuity and invention to create special effects. With the advent of filmmaking came new challenges in makeup design—artists were required to create makeup that would not only hold up under intense lighting, but would look realistic close up. The silent film star Lon Chaney was a pioneer in makeup effects; his dedication to the craft was so extreme that he permanently injured himself with the restrictive prosthetics he used in *The Hunchback of Notre Dame* in 1923. His gruesome makeup design for *The Phantom of the Opera* in 1925 set a standard for all horror films to follow; today, the horror genre has inspired some of the most inventive and memorable makeup effects in film history.

THE JOB

Some of makeup artist Vincent Guastini's creations have involved turning Alanis Morissette into God and Matt Damon and Ben Affleck into angels. These effects for the film *Dogma* hearken back to the earliest examples of theatrical makeup, back to the Middle Ages when makeup effects were used to represent God, angels, and devils. But Guastini did not rely on the simple symbolic face painting of the past; this production demanded that he design complicated animatronic wings, detailed rubber masks, and radio-controlled mechanical creatures. With a crew of some of the top makeup artists in the business, Guastini created effects using rubber, plastic, fiberglass, latex paints, radio-control units from model airplanes, and steel cables. "As well as," Guastini says, "the old standby of a makeup kit filled with grease paints, makeup, rubber glues, brushes, and powders."

From a seven-foot-tall alien for the film *Metamorphosis: The Alien Factor* to the animatronic killer doll Chucky in *Child's Play III*, Guastini has created some very bizarre and disturbing effects. "Movies like *Star Wars* and horror movies left an impact on me as a kid," Guastini says, citing his inspirations. He is also called upon to create less extreme transformations with makeup; his production company worked on *The Last of the Mohicans*, which involved applying wounds and prosthetics to hundreds of actors and extras.

Not every project involves prosthetics and special effects. Makeup artists also apply "clean" makeup, which is a technique of applying foundations and powders to keep actors and models looking natural under the harsh lighting of stage and film productions. Makeup artists accent, or downplay, an actor's natural features. They conceal an actor's scars, skin blemishes, tattoos, and wrinkles, as well as apply these things when needed for the character. Having read the script and met with the director and technicians, makeup artists take into consideration many factors: the age of the characters, the setting of the production, the time period, lighting effects, and other details that determine how an actor should appear. Historical productions require a great deal of research to learn about the hair and clothing styles of the time. Makeup artists also style hair; apply wigs, bald caps, beards, and sideburns; and temporarily color hair. In many states, however, makeup artists are limited in the hair services they can perform; some productions bring in locally licensed cosmetologists for hair cutting, dye jobs, and perms.

After much preparation, the makeup artist becomes an important backstage presence during a production. Throughout the making of a film, makeup artists arrive early for work every day. On the set of *Dogma,* preparing an actor's makeup took four to six hours. "We were always the first to arrive and the last to leave the set," Guastini says of his crew of artists. Makeup artists are required to maintain the actors' proper makeup throughout filming and to help the actors remove the makeup at the end of the day. With the aid of fluorescent lighting, makeup artists apply the makeup, and they keep their eyes on the monitors during filming to make sure the makeup looks right. Guastini's production crew is also responsible for the mechanical creatures they create. "We must do constant repairs and upkeep on any mechanical creatures, making sure they're in working order," Guastini says.

Most makeup artists for film are in business for themselves, contracting work from studios, production companies, and special effects houses on a freelance basis. They may supplement their film work with projects for TV, video, commercials, industrial films, the fashion industry, the cosmetics industry, and photo shoots for professional photographers. Makeup artists for theater may also work freelance or be employed full time by a theater or theater troupe. Makeup artists for theater find work with regional theaters, touring shows, and recreational parks.

REQUIREMENTS
High School
Does becoming a makeup artist sound interesting to you? If so, there are a number of classes you can take in high school to help prepare you for this profession. Take all the art classes you can, including art history if this is offered at your school. Photography courses will help you understand the use of light and shadow. Courses in illustration, painting, and drawing will help you to develop the skills you'll need for illustrating proposed makeup effects. Learning about sculpting is important, as creating special makeup effects with rubber, prosthetics, and glue is often much like sculpting from clay. Other helpful

Makeup artists work to turn a male actor into a female for a movie.
(*The Image Works*)

classes for you to take are anatomy and chemistry. Anatomy will give you an understanding of the human body, and chemistry will give you insight into the products you will be using. If your school offers drama classes, be sure to take these. In drama class you will gain an understanding of all the different elements—such as scripts, actors, and location—needed for a production. Computer classes will give you exposure to this technology, which you may use in the future to design projects. Try experimenting with makeup and special effects on your own. Take photographs of your efforts in order to build a portfolio of your work. Finally, because this work is typically done on a freelance basis and you will need to manage your business accounts, it will be helpful for you to take math, business, and accounting classes.

Postsecondary Training

There are a number of postsecondary educational routes you can take to become a makeup artist. If you have experience and a portfolio to show off your work, you may be able to enter the business right out of high school. This route is not always advisable, however, because your chances for establishing a successful freelance career without further training are slim. You must be very ambitious, enthusiastic, and capable of seeking out successful mentors willing to teach you the ropes. This can mean a lot of time working for free or for very little pay.

Another route you can take is to get specific training for makeup artistry through vocational schools. One advantage of this route is that after graduating from the program, you will be able to use the school's career services office, instructors, and other graduates as possible networking sources for jobs. Probably the most highly respected schools for makeup artists in film are the Joe Blasco Professional Make-Up Artist Training Centers, which have several locations across the country. Topics you might study at a Joe Blasco school include beauty makeup, old age makeup, bald cap, hairwork, and monster makeup. Some people in the business have cosmetology degrees, also offered by vocational schools. A cosmetology course of study, however, is not typically geared toward preparing you for makeup artistry work in the entertainment industry.

A third route you can take is to get a broad-based college or university education that results in either a bachelor's or master's degree. Popular majors for makeup artists include theater, art history, film history, photography, and fashion merchandising. In addition to makeup courses, it is important to take classes in painting, illustration, computer design, and animation. A master of fine arts degree in theater or filmmaking will allow you to gain hands-on experience in production as well as working with a faculty of practicing artists.

Other Requirements

Patience and the ability to get along well with people are important for a makeup artist—throughout a film production, the actors will spend many hours in the makeup chair. Though many actors will be easy to work with, you may have to put up with much irritability, as well as overwhelming egos. Producers and directors can also be difficult to work with. And, as you gain more experience, you may have more knowledge about filmmaking than some of the producers of the projects. This may put you in frustrating situations, and you may see time wasted in costly mistakes.

Attention to detail is important; you must be quick to spot any makeup problems before they are filmed. Such responsibilities can be stressful—a whole production team will be relying on you to properly apply makeup that will look good on film. If your work isn't up to par, the whole production will suffer. Work as a makeup artist requires as much creativity and ingenuity as any other filmmaking task. The directors and actors rely on the makeup artists to come up with interesting makeup effects and solutions to filming problems. "It's important to be original in your work," Vincent Guastini advises. Guastini is also an example of the importance of ambition and dedication—within five years of graduating high school, he began work on his first motion picture. A year after that first assignment, he had developed a list of clients and put together a team of special effects artists. Because of the tough, competitive nature of the entertainment industry, makeup artists must be persistent and enthusiastic in their pursuit of work.

As a makeup artist, you may want to consider joining a union. The International Alliance of Theatrical Stage Employees, Moving Picture Technicians, Artists and Allied Crafts of the United States, Its Territories, and Canada represents workers in theater, film, and television production. Hair stylists, makeup artists, engineers, art directors, and set designers are some of the professionals who belong to the 500 local unions affiliated with the alliance. Union membership is not required of most makeup artists for film and theater, but it can help individuals negotiate better wages, benefits, and working conditions. Theaters in larger cities may require union membership of makeup artists, while smaller, regional theaters across the country are less likely to require membership.

EXPLORING

High school drama departments or local community theaters can provide you with great opportunities to explore the makeup artist's work. Volunteer to assist with makeup during a stage production and you will learn about the materials and tools of a makeup kit, as well as see your work under stage lights. A high school video production team or film department may also offer you opportunities for makeup experience.

Most states have their own film commissions that are responsible for promoting film locales and inviting film productions to the local area. These film commissions generally need volunteers and may have internships for students. By working for a film commission, you will learn about productions coming to your state and may have the chance to work on the production. Film industry publications such as *Variety* (http://www.variety.com) can alert you to internship opportunities.

The summer is a great time for students interested in stage production to gain firsthand experience. There are probably local productions in your area, but summer theaters often promote positions nationally. The Theatre Communications Group publishes a directory of nonprofit professional theaters across the country. Its bimonthly publication, *ARTSEARCH,* provides information on summer theater positions and internships.

Finally, explore this career by reading other publications for the field. For example, check out *Make-Up Artist Magazine* (http://www. makeupmag.com), a bimonthly publication with profiles of makeup artists for film as well as how-to columns and product information.

EMPLOYERS

There are approximately 2,000 makeup artists employed in the United States. Although makeup artists work in a wide variety of circumstances, from theater and the cosmetics industry to television and movies, they usually are self-employed, contracting individual jobs. Theater troupes, touring shows, and amusement parks may hire staff makeup artists, but in the film industry, makeup artists work on a freelance basis. Large cities and metropolitan areas will provide the majority of jobs for makeup artists, particularly those cities associated with thriving theaters, movie or television studios, fashion photography, and modeling/talent agencies. Although there may be some jobs in smaller towns, they probably will be mostly along the lines of industrial films, corporate videos, and photographic shoots—not very promising for those who wish to make a living in this line of work. Those who aspire to work exclusively as makeup artists gravitate toward the big cities.

STARTING OUT

You should keep a photographic record of all the work you do for theater and film productions, including photos of any drawings or sculptures you have done for art classes. It's important to have a portfolio to send along with your resume to effects shops, makeup departments, and producers. "Be prepared to work for free or for little money at the start," Vincent Guastini advises, "just to hook up with the right person who will hire you the next time out." To build up a portfolio of photographs, experiment in art classes and at home with makeup and special effects, and photograph the results. Check with local TV studios about work in their makeup departments. Locally produced newscasts, children's programming, documentaries, and commercials offer opportunities for makeup artists. Commercials are often quick productions (between one and three days) with small casts, and they pay well. Department stores hire makeup artists to demonstrate and sell cosmetic products, which may be a starting position for those who want to earn a salary while getting on-the-job training and practice.

Because of the freelance nature of the business, you will be going from project to project. This requires you to constantly seek out work.

Read industry trade magazines like *Variety,* and don't be shy about submitting your portfolio to producers and studios. Self-promotion will be an important part of your success as a makeup artist.

ADVANCEMENT

Many makeup artists start as assistants or volunteers on a production, making contacts and connections. They eventually take on projects for which they are in charge of makeup departments and designing makeup effects. They may also establish their own production companies and make their own films or stage their own plays. "I would love to direct someday," Vincent Guastini says about his future, "or produce a film, but the project the first time out should be a really solid, visually exciting film that incorporates my current talents."

Successful, experienced makeup artists can pick and choose their projects and work as much as they like. In the early years, makeup artists must frequently take on a variety of different projects just for the money; however, as they become established in the field and develop a solid reputation, they can concentrate on projects specific to their interests.

EARNINGS

Makeup artists usually contract with a production, negotiating a daily rate. This rate can vary greatly from project to project, depending on the budget of the production, the prestige of the project, and other factors. Even well-established makeup artists occasionally forgo payment to work on the low-budget independent productions of filmmakers they respect.

Independent contractors don't draw steady, yearly salaries. This means they may work long hours for several weeks, then, upon completion of a production, go without work for several weeks. Unless makeup artists are part of the union, they may be without benefits, having to provide all their own health insurance. An experienced makeup artist can make around $300 a day on a film with a sizable budget; some of the top makeup artists in the business command around $1,000 a day. Theatrical makeup artists can make comparable daily wages on Broadway, or in a theater in a large city; some small theaters, however, may only pay around $50 a day.

Because of such variables as the unsteady nature of the work, the makeup artist's experience, and even where he or she works, the yearly incomes for these individuals vary widely. Some makeup artists may show yearly earnings little higher than those resulting from the minimum wage. Others may have annual income in the hundreds of thousands of dollars. The U.S. Department of Labor reports that makeup artists, theatrical and performance, had median annual salaries of $23,480 in 2005. Salaries ranged from less than $13,870 to more than $68,900.

WORK ENVIRONMENT

Long hours, deadlines, and tight budgets can result in high stress on a movie set. Because makeup artists move from production to production, they work with different groups of people all the time, and in different locales and settings. Although this allows makeup artists the opportunity to travel, it may also make a makeup artist feel displaced. While working on a production, they may have to forgo a social life, working long hours to design effects and prepare the actors for filming. The workdays may be twice as long as in the average workplace, and those work hours may be a stressful combination of working hurriedly and then waiting.

For those passionate about the work, however, any uncomfortable or frustrating conditions are easily overlooked. "I like creating something from nothing and seeing it alive and moving," Vincent Guastini says in regard to the creatures he has constructed for special effects. He also appreciates the travel and variety. "I like the people I meet," he says, "and the job is always different no matter the project or effect."

When working for the theater, the conditions are generally more controlled. With the exception of outdoor productions, theatrical makeup artists work in the dressing and makeup rooms of theaters and concert halls. The work can be very stressful, however, as the actors hurry to prepare for live productions.

OUTLOOK

Makeup artists will find their opportunities increasing in the film and television industries. Digital TV has made it possible for hundreds of cable channels to be piped into homes. The original programming needed to fill the schedules of these new channels results in jobs for makeup artists. Makeup effects artists will find challenging and well-paying work as the film industry pushes the envelope on special effects. These makeup artists may be using computers more and more, as digital design becomes an important tool in creating film effects.

Funding for theaters, some of which comes from the National Endowment for the Arts, is always limited and may be reduced during economic downturns or when productions are unpopular. During these times many theaters may be unable to hire the cast and crew needed for new productions. There has been a revived interest in Broadway, however, due to highly successful musicals like *Rent, The Lion King,* and *Wicked.* This interest could result in better business for traveling productions, as well as regional theaters across the country.

There will be a continuing need for makeup artists in still photography to prepare models for catalog and magazine shoots. The *Occupational Outlook Handbook* reports that employment opportunities for theatrical and performance makeup artists will grow about as fast as the average for all occupations through 2014.

FOR MORE INFORMATION

For information on the alliance, a union representing more than 100,000 members in entertainment and related fields in the United States and Canada, contact

International Alliance of Theatrical Stage Employees, Moving Picture Technicians, Artists and Allied Crafts of the United States, Its Territories, and Canada
1430 Broadway, 20th Floor
New York, NY 10018-3348
Tel: 212-730-1770
http://www.iatse-intl.org

For information about how to order a copy of or subscription to Make-Up Artist Magazine, *contact*

Make-Up Artist Magazine
4018 NE 112th Avenue, Suite D-8
Vancouver, WA 98682-5703
Tel: 800-805-6648
http://www.makeupmag.com

For information about jobs and a sample copy of ARTSEARCH, *contact*

Theatre Communications Group
520 Eighth Avenue, 24th Floor
New York, NY 10018-4156
Tel: 212-609-5900
Email: tcg@tcg.org
http://www.tcg.org

For information about the Joe Blasco schools and careers in makeup artistry, visit

Joe Blasco Professional Make-Up Artist Training Centers
http://www.joeblasco.com

Massage Therapists

OVERVIEW

Massage therapy is a broad term referring to a number of health-related practices, including Swedish massage, sports massage, Rolfing, Shiatsu and acupressure, trigger point therapy, and reflexology. Although the techniques vary, most *massage therapists* (or *massotherapists*) press and rub the skin and muscles. Relaxed muscles, improved blood circulation and joint mobility, reduced stress and anxiety, and decreased recovery time for sprains and injured muscles are just a few of the potential benefits of massage therapy. Massage therapists are sometimes called *bodyworkers*. The titles *masseur* and *masseuse,* once common, are now rare among those who use massage for therapy and rehabilitation. There are approximately 97,000 massage therapists employed in the United States.

HISTORY

Getting a massage used to be considered a luxury reserved only for the very wealthy, or an occasional splurge for the less affluent. Some people thought massage to be a cover for illicit activities such as prostitution. With increased regulation of certification and a trend toward ergonomics in the home and workplace, however, massage therapy is recognized as an important tool in both alternative and preventative health care. Regular massage can help alleviate physical ailments faced by people today: physical stress brought on by an increase in sedentary lifestyle, aches and pains from hours spent in front of the computer, as well as injuries of the weekend warrior trying to make up for five days of inactivity.

QUICK FACTS

School Subjects
Health
Physical education

Personal Skills
Helping/teaching
Mechanical/manipulative

Work Environment
Primarily indoors
Primarily one location

Minimum Education Level
Some postsecondary training

Salary Range
$15,000 to $32,890 to
$71,060+

Certification or Licensing
Recommended (certification)
Required by certain states
(licensing)

Outlook
Faster than the average

DOT
334

GOE
14.06.01

NOC
3235

O*NET-SOC
31-9011.00

THE JOB

Massage therapists work to produce physical, mental, and emotional benefits through the manipulation of the body's soft tissue. Auxiliary methods, such as the movement of joints and the application of dry and steam heat, are also used. Among the potential physical benefits are the release of muscle tension and stiffness, reduced blood pressure, better blood circulation, a shorter healing time for sprains and pulled muscles, increased flexibility and greater range of motion in the joints, and reduced swelling from edema (excess fluid buildup in body tissue). Massage may also improve posture, strengthen the immune system, and reduce the formation of scar tissue.

Mental and emotional benefits include a relaxed state of mind, reduced stress and anxiety, clearer thinking, and a general sense of well-being. Physical, mental, and emotional health are all interconnected: Being physically fit and healthy can improve emotional health, just as a positive mental attitude can bolster the immune system to help the body fight off infection. A release of muscle tension also leads to reduced stress and anxiety, and physical manipulation of sore muscles can help speed the healing process.

There are many different approaches a massage therapist may take. Among the most popular are Swedish massage, sports massage, Rolfing, Shiatsu and acupressure, and trigger point therapy.

In Swedish massage the traditional techniques are effleurage, petrissage, friction, and tapotement. Effleurage (stroking) uses light and hard rhythmic strokes to relax muscles and improve blood circulation. It is often performed at the beginning and end of a massage session. Petrissage (kneading) is the rhythmic squeezing, pressing, and lifting of a muscle. For friction, the fingers, thumb, or palm or heel of the hand are pressed into the skin with a small circular movement. The massage therapist's fingers are sometimes pressed deeply into a joint. Tapotement (tapping), in which the hands strike the skin in rapid succession, is used to improve blood circulation.

During the session the client, covered with sheets, lies undressed on a padded table. Oil or lotion is used to smooth the skin. Some massage therapists use aromatherapy, adding fragrant essences to the oil to relax the client and stimulate circulation. Swedish massage may employ a number of auxiliary techniques, including the use of rollers, belts, and vibrators; steam and dry heat; ultraviolet and infrared light; and saunas, whirlpools, steam baths, and packs of hot water or ice.

Sports massage is essentially Swedish massage used in the context of athletics. A light massage generally is given before an event or

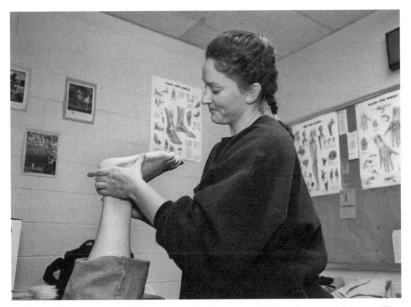

A therapist massages the sprained ankle of a high school athlete. *(The Image Works)*

game to loosen and warm the muscles. This reduces the chance of injury and may improve performance. After the event the athlete is massaged more deeply to alleviate pain, reduce stiffness, and promote healing.

Rolfing, developed by American Ida Rolf, involves deep, sometimes painful massage. Intense pressure is applied to various parts of the body. Rolfing practitioners believe that emotional disturbances, physical pain, and other problems can occur when the body is out of alignment—for example, as a result of poor posture. This method takes 10 sessions to complete.

Like the ancient Oriental science of acupuncture, Shiatsu and acupressure are based on the concept of meridians, or invisible channels of flowing energy in the body. The massage therapist presses down on particular points along these channels to release blocked energy and untie knots of muscle tension. For this approach the patient wears loosely fitted clothes, lies on the floor or on a futon, and is not given oil or lotion for the skin.

Trigger point therapy, a neuromuscular technique, focuses in on a painful area, or trigger point, in a muscle. A trigger point might be associated with a problem in another part of the body. Using the fingers or an instrument, such as a rounded piece of wood, concentrated pressure is placed on the irritated area in order to "deactivate" the trigger point.

All of these methods of massage can be altered and intermingled depending on the client's needs. Massage therapists can be proficient in one or many of the methods, and usually tailor a session to the individual.

REQUIREMENTS

High School

Since massage therapists need to know more than just technical skills, many practitioners use the basic knowledge learned in high school as a foundation to build a solid career in the field. During your high school years, you should take fundamental science courses, such as chemistry, anatomy, and biology. These classes will give you a basic understanding of the human body and prepare you for the health and anatomy classes you will take while completing your postsecondary education. English, psychology, and other classes relating to communications and human development will also be useful as the successful massage therapist is able to express his or her ideas with clients as well as understand the clients' reactions to the therapy. If you think you might wish to run your own massage therapy business someday, computer and business courses are essential. Finally, do not neglect your own physical well-being. Take physical education and health courses to strengthen your body and your understanding of your own conditioning.

Postsecondary Training

The best way to become a successful massage therapist is to attend an accredited massage therapy school after you have finished high school. There are approximately 300 state-accredited massage schools located throughout the United States. More than 80 of these schools are accredited or approved by the Commission on Massage Therapy Accreditation (COMTA), a major accrediting agency for massage therapy programs and an affiliate of the American Massage Therapy Association (AMTA). COMTA-accredited and -approved schools must provide at least 500 hours of classroom instruction. Studies should include such courses as anatomy, physiology, theory and practice of massage therapy, and ethics. In addition, students should receive supervised hands-on experience. Most programs offer students the opportunity to participate at clinics, such as those providing massage services at hospices, hospitals, and shelters, or at school clinics that are open to the general public.

Massage therapy training programs typically take about a year to complete. Students can specialize in particular disciplines, such as infant massage or rehabilitative massage. Basic first aid and cardio-pulmonary resuscitation (CPR) must also be learned. When choosing a school, you should pay close attention to the philosophy and curricula of the program, since a wide range of program options exists. Also, keep in mind that licensure requirements for massage therapists vary by state. For example, some state medical boards require students to have completed more than 500 hours of instruction before they can be recognized as massage therapists. Part of your process for choosing a school, therefore, should include making sure that the school's curriculum will allow you to meet your state's requirements.

Certification or Licensing

Currently, 37 states and the District of Columbia regulate the practice of massage therapy, requiring licensure, certification, or registration. Because requirements for licensing, certification, registration, and even local ordinances vary, however, you will need to check with your state's department of regulatory agencies to get specifics for your area. Typically, requirements include completing an accredited program and passing a written test and a demonstration of massage therapy techniques.

The National Certification Board for Therapeutic Massage and Bodywork offers two national certification examinations for massage therapists: the National Certification Examination for Therapeutic Massage and Bodywork and the National Certification Examination for Therapeutic Massage. To learn more about each exam, visit http://www.ncbtmb.com. Certification is highly recommended, since it demonstrates a therapist's high-level of education and achievement. Certification may also make a therapist a more desirable candidate for job openings.

Other Requirements

Physical requirements of massage therapists generally include the ability to use their hands and other tools to rub or press on the client's body. Manual dexterity is usually required to administer the treatments, as is the ability to stand for at least an hour at a time. Special modifications or accommodations can often be made for people with different abilities.

If you are interested in becoming a massage therapist, you should be, above all, nurturing and caring. Constance Bickford, a certified massage therapist in Chicago, thinks that it is necessary to be both flexible and creative: easily adaptable to the needs of the client, as well as able to use different techniques to help the client feel better. Listening well and responding to the client is vital, as is focusing all attention on the task at hand. Massage therapists need to tune in to their client rather than zone out, thinking about the grocery list or what to cook for supper. An effective massage is a mindful one, where massage therapist and client work together toward improved health.

To be a successful massage therapist, you should also be trustworthy and sensitive. Someone receiving a massage may feel awkward lying naked in an office covered by a sheet, listening to music while a stranger kneads his or her muscles. A good massage therapist will make the client feel comfortable in what could potentially be perceived as a vulnerable situation.

Therapists considering opening up their own business should be prepared for busy and slow times. In order to both serve their clients well and stay in business, they should be adequately staffed during rush seasons, and must be financially able to withstand dry spells.

EXPLORING

The best way to become familiar with massage therapy is to get a massage. Look for a certified therapist in your area and make an appointment for a session. If you can afford it, consider going to several different therapists who offer different types of massage. Also, ask if you can set up an informational interview with one of the therapists. Explain that you are interested in pursuing this career and come to the interview prepared to ask questions. What is this massage therapist's educational background? Why was he or she drawn to the job? What is the best part of this work? By talking to a massage therapist, you may also have the chance to develop a mentoring relationship with him or her.

A less costly approach is to find a book on massage instruction at a local public library or bookstore. Massage techniques can then be practiced at home. Books on self-massage are available. Many books discuss in detail the theoretical basis for the techniques. Videos that demonstrate massage techniques are available as well.

Consider volunteering at a hospice, nursing home, or shelter. This work will give you experience in caring for others and help you develop good listening skills. It is important for massage therapists to listen well and respond appropriately to their clients' needs. The massage therapist must make clients feel comfortable, and volunteer work can help foster the skills necessary to achieve this.

EMPLOYERS

Approximately 97,000 massage therapists are employed in the United States. After graduating from an accredited school of massage therapy, there are a number of possibilities for employment. Doctors' offices, hospitals, clinics, health clubs, resorts, country clubs, cruise ships, community service organizations, and nursing homes, for example, all employ massage therapists. Some chiropractors have a massage therapist on staff to whom they can refer patients. A number of massage therapists run their own businesses. Most opportunities for work will be in larger, urban areas with population growth, although massage therapy is slowly spreading to more rural areas as well.

STARTING OUT

There are a number of resources you can use to locate a job. The AMTA offers job placement information to certified massage therapists who belong to the organization. Massage therapy schools have career services offices. Newspapers often list jobs. Some graduates are able to enter the field as self-employed massage therapists, scheduling their own appointments and managing their own offices.

Networking is a valuable tool in maintaining a successful massage therapy enterprise. Many massage therapists get clients through referrals, and often rely on word of mouth to build a solid customer base. Beginning massage therapists might wish to consult businesses about arranging onsite massage sessions for their employees.

Health fairs are also good places to distribute information about massage therapy practices and learn about other services in the industry. Often, organizers of large sporting events will employ massage therapists to give massages to athletes at the finish line. These events may include marathons and runs or bike rides held to raise money for charitable organizations.

ADVANCEMENT

For self-employed massage therapists, advancement is measured by reputation, the ability to attract clients, and the fees charged for services. Health clubs, country clubs, and other institutions have supervisory positions for massage therapists. In a community service organization, massage therapists may be promoted to the position of health service director. Licensed massage therapists often become instructors or advisers at schools for massage therapy.

They may also make themselves available to advise individuals or companies on the short- and long-term benefits of massage therapy, and how massage therapy can be introduced into professional work environments.

EARNINGS

The earnings of massage therapists vary greatly with the level of experience and location of practice. Therapists in New York and California, for example, typically charge higher rates than those in other parts of the country. Some entry-level massage therapists earn as little as minimum wage, but with experience, a massage therapist can charge from $45 to $70 for a one-hour session.

The U.S. Department of Labor reports that massage therapists earned a median salary of $32,890 a year in 2005. The lowest 10 percent earned $15,000 or less, while the highest 10 percent earned $71,060 or more.

An article in *USA Today* profiling the career of massage therapist reported hourly earnings ranging from $40 to $110. Those with earnings at the high end typically worked in higher paying geographic areas (such as large cities), had years of experience, and had built up a large clientele. For therapists who worked in spas, salons, resorts, and gyms, *USA Today* noted earnings of $10 to $30 per hour, plus tips (which can add thousands of dollars to annual incomes). For massage therapists working full time, the article estimated yearly earnings of approximately $35,000 to $40,000. Well-established therapists who manage to schedule an average of 20 clients a week for one-hour sessions can earn more than $40,000 annually.

Approximately two-thirds of all massage therapists are self-employed, and self-employed therapists are not paid for the time spent on bookkeeping, maintaining their offices, waiting for customers to arrive, and looking for new clients. In addition, they must pay a self-employment tax and provide their own benefits. With membership in some national organizations, self-employed massage therapists may be eligible for group life, health, liability, and renter's insurance through the organization's insurance agency.

Massage therapists employed by a health club usually get free or discounted memberships to the club. Those who work for resorts or on cruise ships can get free or discounted travel and accommodations, in addition to full access to facilities when not on duty. Massage therapists employed by a sports team often get to attend the team's sporting events.

WORK ENVIRONMENT

Massage therapists work in clean, comfortable settings. Because a relaxed environment is essential, the massage room may be dim, and soft music, scents, and oils are often used. Since massage therapists may see a number of people per day, it is important to maintain a hygienic working area. This involves changing sheets on the massage table after each client, as well as cleaning and sterilizing any implements used, and washing hands frequently.

Massage therapists employed by businesses may use a portable massage chair—that is, a padded chair that leaves the client in a forward-leaning position ideal for massage of the back and neck. Some massage therapists work out of their homes or travel to the homes of their clients.

The workweek of a massage therapist is typically 35 to 40 hours, which may include evenings and weekends. On average, 20 hours or fewer per week are spent with clients, and the other hours are spent making appointments and taking care of other business-related details.

Since the physical work is sometimes demanding, massage therapists need to take measures to prevent repetitive stress disorders, such as carpal tunnel syndrome. Also, for their own personal safety, massage therapists who work out of their homes or have odd office hours need to be particularly careful about scheduling appointments with unknown clients.

OUTLOOK

The U.S. Department of Labor predicts a strong employment outlook for massage therapists through 2014. The growing acceptance of massage therapy as an important health care discipline has led to the creation of additional jobs for massage therapists in many sectors.

One certified massage therapist points to sports massage as one of the fastest growing specialties in the field. The increasing popularity of professional sports has given massage therapists new opportunities to work as key members of a team's staff. Their growing presence in sports has made massage therapy more visible to the public, spreading the awareness of the physical benefits of massage.

Massages aren't just for athletes. According to a survey by the American Massage Therapy Association, 22 percent of Americans surveyed in August 2005 had a massage in the past 12 months. The survey found that people are getting massages not just for medical reasons, but to relax and reduce stress.

There is a growing opportunity for massage therapists in the corporate world. Many employers eager to hold on to good employees offer perks, such as workplace massages. As a result, many massage therapists are working as mobile business consultants.

FOR MORE INFORMATION

For information on careers and education programs, contact
American Massage Therapy Association
500 Davis Street
Evanston, IL 60201-4668
Tel: 877-905-2700
Email: info@amtamassage.org
http://www.amtamassage.org

For information on careers in the field, state board requirements, and training programs, contact the following:
Associated Bodywork and Massage Professionals
1271 Sugarbush Drive
Evergreen, CO 80439-9766
Tel: 800-458-2267
Email: expectmore@abmp.com
http://www.abmp.com

Massagetherapy.com
http://www.massagetherapy.com

For information on accreditation and programs, contact
Commission on Massage Therapy Accreditation
1007 Church Street, Suite 302
Evanston, IL 60201-5912
Tel: 847-869-5039
Email: info@comta.org
http://www.comta.org

For information about state certification and education requirements, contact
National Certification Board for Therapeutic Massage and
　Bodywork
1901 South Meyers Road, Suite 240
Oakbrook Terrace, IL 60181-5243
Tel: 800-296-0664
Email: info@ncbtmb.com
http://www.ncbtmb.com

Mortuary Cosmetologists

OVERVIEW

A *mortuary cosmetologist* is a licensed cosmetologist who performs a variety of cosmetic services to prepare a deceased person for funeral services. Sometimes called *desairologists*, mortuary cosmetologists are trained to use products to style or alter the hair, face, and nails to prepare a deceased person for viewing and/or burial. In doing so, mortuary cosmetologists may provide comfort to grieving families and friends by making their deceased loved one appear as they wish them to be remembered. Mortuary cosmetologists are primarily cosmetologists who provide this additional service when requested, although full-time careers can be made of mortuary cosmetology. Approximately 670,000 cosmetologists, hairdressers, hairstylists, and barbers are employed in the United States.

HISTORY

In all societies, human bodies are prepared in some fashion before they are laid to rest. Archaeologists have discovered that the practice of preparing the dead dates back to the earliest Homo sapien groups. The Neanderthals stained their dead with red ocher, a possible indication of some belief in afterlife. Throughout history, preparation of the dead has varied across cultures, but most practices included washing the body, dressing it in special garments, and adorning it with ornaments, religious objects, or mementos. Most of these practices continue throughout the world today.

Contemporary anthropological studies interpret funeral customs as symbolic expressions of the values that prevail in a particular society. In the United States, presentation of the body so that it appears natural and comfortable for its last public appearance is a part of the ritual.

Mortuary cosmetology as a career choice is fairly new, according to Noella C. Charest-Papagno, a practicing mortuary cosmetologist and author. Cosmetic preparation of the deceased is not a service that has evolved only with the mortuary cosmetologist. Funeral directors and embalmers have traditionally provided these services. As part of their licensing requirements, these professionals must be able to perform all preparations necessary—including applying makeup and styling hair. In many cases, the standard flesh-tone makeup is all that is needed. Those who had simple hairstyles, especially men, may not require the specialized services of a cosmetologist.

Mortuary cosmetology as a specialty was really only recognized in the late 1970s and early 1980s. Thanks to the efforts of Charest-Papagno and other cosmetology professionals, the funeral and cosmetology industries have come to realize that there is no reason why people who were particular about their appearance in life shouldn't have the same service available to them in death.

Today more schools are offering classes on mortuary cosmetology; they were unheard of in cosmetology schools a few decades ago. Charest-Papagno has published a book, *Handbook of Desairology for Cosmetologists Servicing Funeral Homes* (J J Publishing, 1996). In that book, Charest-Papagno coined the term *desairology* (from the words deceased and hair), and many in the field prefer it to mortuary cosmetology.

THE JOB

Making the deceased appear as they did in life—the way their families want them to be remembered—is no small task. Occasionally, mortuary cosmetologists are asked to perform cosmetic services on a person they knew, often a client. But more frequently, mortuary cosmetologists work from a photograph provided by the family. Each situation is different—the quality of the photograph, difficulty of the style requested, conditions of death such as illness or trauma, and chemicals used in preparation of the body can all make the mortuary cosmetologist's job easier or more difficult.

Sterilizing and embalming chemicals used by funeral home personnel add to the dehydration process that occurs on a body, making the hair very dry and brittle. Also, the hair of decedents who were on medication before their deaths can be very thin and fall out easily when the cosmetologist attempts to cut or style it. In addition to these factors, the simple fact that the person who is being styled is in a horizontal rather than vertical position can be a challenge to a beginning mortuary cosmetologist. Denice Lafferty, a mortuary cosmetologist for more than 14 years, recalls that learning to roll hair the opposite direction to get it to set right was one of her biggest early challenges.

Getting over her uneasiness around the deceased was another challenge, Lafferty says, but it was something she grew accustomed to quicker than she expected. Her first mortuary job was for an elderly client she had grown close to. She styled the woman's hair regularly and visited her in the hospital before she died.

"I was scared to death the first time I was asked, but you have to keep in mind that this is the last thing you can do for this person. They [the family] have put their trust in you," Lafferty says.

Despite the seemingly gloomy nature of the work, Lafferty notes the job is not without its rewards. "It's something you can't be prepared for, working with the dead. But after a while it doesn't bother you when you see what a valuable service you are providing. I get cards, thank you's, personal phone calls, and it makes you feel good that you were able to do that for somebody," she says.

As with most health care and funeral professionals, the initial experience dealing with the deceased usually evokes uneasiness. However, as mortuary cosmetologists gain more experience, the knowledge of the comfort they may provide to a grieving family generally helps offset their own discomfort. Also with experience comes a natural focus on the task at hand. Most mortuary cosmetologists are too busy to dwell on morbid thoughts; rather, their focus is on doing their job well for the sake of the family and the memory of the deceased. In general, mortuary cosmetologists do not handle the deceased beyond the preparations they are asked to make to the hair, face, or nails.

Requests for desairology services for deceased men are infrequent. On occasion, mortuary cosmetologists may be requested for a deceased man, based on the family's request or a trauma or illness requiring camouflage makeup.

Because the pores open after death, a transparent pancake makeup is applied to all deceased—men and women alike—in preparation for viewing. This makeup is generally applied by funeral home personnel, not the mortuary cosmetologist.

Most jobs are paid on a commission basis. In many cases, the funeral home bills the deceased's family for all services provided, even if the funeral home didn't directly provide them—including cosmetology services—so the family has just one bill to worry about. This also is done because the Federal Trade Commission requires funeral homes to disclose their fees to consumers on a general price list. The list includes the category "Other Preparation of Body," which means any preparation made to make the body presentable, including dressing, placing in casket, hair cutting, styling, and makeup.

Mortuary cosmetologists find clients in many different ways. If a mortuary cosmetologist has a relationship with a funeral home, the funeral home director may recommend him or her to a client who inquires about such services. Other clients may hear about a mortuary cosmetologist from their own beauticians, who may not provide such services. Also, mortuary cosmetologists seeking clients may find that listing their services in the yellow pages under funeral services is helpful, as well as leaving their business cards with salons that don't have a mortuary cosmetologist on staff. Mortuary cosmetologists often work as traditional cosmetologists in salons, malls, department stores, nursing homes, and beauty supply stores.

REQUIREMENTS

High School

People outside the field of cosmetology are often surprised at the diverse subjects that cosmetology students must learn. High school classes that are also part of a college preparatory curriculum will help you if you plan to pursue this career. Science classes, such as physics, chemistry, and biology, will give you a background that you will find valuable years down the road—both in cosmetology school, when you learn specifically how those disciplines apply to the trade, and as a practicing cosmetologist, when you will use your knowledge to solve problems independently. In addition to science classes, mathematics courses such as algebra and geometry will give you preparation in working with numbers and formulas. Again, these are skills you will use in your later career. Of course, classes such as English and speech will allow you to practice communication skills that will be important when you deal with a wide variety of people, some of whom will be experiencing a range of emotions. Also, because there is the possibility that you will be dealing with grieving families and friends of the deceased, consider taking psychology courses that will give you a greater understanding of people's reaction to stress and grief. Finally, if you have the opportunity, take art classes that give you a chance to work with design and color.

Several high schools in the United States offer cosmetology programs as part of their vocational curriculum. At one such school,

South Garland High School in Texas, students study bacteriology, electricity, and geometry to help them prepare for this work. Any student planning to pursue a career in cosmetology should keep in mind that most cosmetology schools require a high school diploma or general equivalency diploma and set a minimum age of 16.

Postsecondary Training

Cosmetology schools, still popularly known as beauty schools, prepare students for different careers in cosmetology. Cosmetology schools generally require 1,000 to 1,500 hours of training, which generally can be completed in a year. Many schools have classes starting throughout the year. According to the National Accrediting Commission of Cosmetology Arts and Sciences (NACCAS), no schools currently offer specific program sequences for mortuary cosmetologists. Many schools offer classes on mortuary services as part of their cosmetology curriculum, but states don't require special licensing for mortuary cosmetologists beyond the standard cosmetology license. Cosmetology schools offer training that leads to licenses in cosmetology (the full range of beauty services, including hair, skin, and nails), esthetics (which is limited to skin care, facial hair removal, and makeup), or nail technology (which is limited to care for the nails and cuticles on the hands and feet). Students of cosmetology can expect their curriculum to include classes in hair cutting and styling, permanent waves, tinting, eyebrow arching, facials, corrective makeup, manicuring, and pedicuring. These classes generally have students practice their new skills on mannequins or observe demonstrations. As students advance in their skills, they often practice on each other. Theory classes may include state law, chemistry, salon business management, and sterilization and sanitation. There are cosmetology schools in every state. Currently NACCAS has accredited approximately 1,000 schools that serve more than 100,000 students.

As a rule, general cosmetology internships are part of postsecondary schooling, although they usually are not called internships. Students advance to hands-on training only after they have completed the classroom and theoretical courses. Many cosmetology schools operate their own salons and offer discounted cosmetology services to the public, provided by cosmetology students in a supervised setting. Students observe and perform a specific type and number of procedures on clients to fulfill requirements of the school and the state they wish to practice in. In addition to passing a written exam, most states require a minimum number of hours of training on live subjects. During school "in-salon training," cosmetologists can expect to work at least 100 hours per month. Situations vary, but many cosmetologists-in-training receive a percentage of the fee for their work. Instructors, in addition to supervising techniques, use this time to give hints on building clientele, such as handing out business cards and explaining other services to the client. This practical experience is vital to launching a successful cosmetology career.

Certification or Licensing

All 50 states require cosmetologists to be licensed. A person must be licensed—as a cosmetologist, funeral director, or embalmer—to perform cosmetic services on the deceased. In many funeral homes, unless the family requests special services or a certain cosmetologist, funeral home personnel do the necessary cosmetic preparations. Most mortuary schools require a class on restorative art that includes basic hair styling and makeup techniques. Restorative art also covers more difficult body preparation work for bodies that have suffered a trauma, such as makeup to camouflage bruises and scrapes or techniques to rebuild a nose.

Only those who have completed the recommended training are permitted to apply for a cosmetology license. Although requirements vary by state, each state requires an application, generally with a minimal fee, and passage of a written examination. The exam determines the applicant's knowledge of pertinent areas such as product chemistry, sanitary rules and regulations, sanitary procedures, chemical service procedures, knowledge of the anatomy of the skin, provisions and requirements of the state in which they wish to practice, and knowledge of labor and compensation laws.

Other Requirements

Cosmetology can be a physically and mentally demanding occupation, and the same applies to mortuary cosmetology. Cosmetologists are on their feet much of the day and their work is very hands-on. Because of the hands-on aspect of the work, mortuary cosmetologists must overcome any fears they may have about working with the dead. Mortuary cosmetologists need to have physical endurance in the shoulders and arms and finger dexterity because much of the time is spent cutting, trimming, or styling hair. Although the mortuary cosmetologist will not be expected to do strenuous physical work, carpal tunnel syndrome, which occurs when damage is done to nerves in the wrist because of repetitive hand motion, is a concern for any cosmetologist. Other helpful attributes for a mortuary cosmetologist to have include a sense of form and balance, the ability to imitate styles if a family has provided pictures of how they want the deceased to appear, and tact and understanding when dealing with families. The mortuary cosmetologist should also have a strong business sense. Since much of this work is done on a freelance basis, the cosmetologist will need to manage his or her finances.

EXPLORING

You can learn more about mortuary cosmetology by checking with local funeral homes, cosmetology schools, and salons. Most professionals are willing to take time to explain their work to students who show an interest. However, the extent to which they can show you the work they do may be limited. In order for an individual to observe cosmetic preparations on the deceased, the decedent's family must give permission. Many families may not be willing to do this. Families are especially reluctant to grant permission to a class, whether it is a high school vocational class or a cosmetology class, to be present for their loved one's preparation. You may have better results approaching a mortuary cosmetologist or funeral home director individually and stating your interest in the field.

EMPLOYERS

Mortuary cosmetologists are rarely employed directly by funeral homes, particularly on a full-time basis. Since this area of cosmetology is relatively new, there generally is not yet a strong enough demand for these services to support full-time mortuary cosmetologists. Most are cosmetologists—either self-employed or employed by a salon—who provide mortuary services on a freelance basis. Many provide services to several funeral homes, especially in more rural areas, where there are fewer people who specialize in this work. In larger cities, one or two large funeral homes that see a high volume may provide enough business for a mortuary cosmetologist to make a part-time or even full-time income. There are approximately 670,000 cosmetologists, hairdressers, hairstylists, and barbers employed in the United States.

STARTING OUT

Few workers are directly involved in preparing the deceased for funerals: directors, embalmers, and cosmetologists. These professionals are the only people who can legally perform these services. Those interested in mortuary cosmetology should consider which aspects of the field appeal to them most in deciding whether to pursue funeral home or cosmetology training. Funeral home training takes longer than cosmetology training. Embalmers generally are required to complete two years of preprofessional college work—

often resulting in an associate's degree. Funeral home directors are required to complete two years of college and then enroll in mortuary school for another year or two.

Those who have completed cosmetology training and are interested in this work should begin by aggressively marketing themselves to local funeral homes. Once the funeral homes know of a cosmetologist in the area who provides these services, they will be able to recommend the cosmetologist for work.

ADVANCEMENT

An article in the salon trade magazine *Techniques* discussed growth areas in the field of cosmetology, including mortuary cosmetology. The article noted that desairology may not hold the glamour of other cosmetology specialties, such as a stage or film artist, but it offers other attractions, such as the opportunity to perform humanitarian services. Mortuary cosmetologists who make funeral homes, salons, and the general public aware of the valuable service they provide can help their businesses grow. Mortuary cosmetologists who build a reputation for providing a valuable service can carve a niche for themselves in their area. Becoming a funeral home's or salon's designated desairologist can lead to steady work, which, because of its specialized nature, generally pays more than regular cosmetology services.

EARNINGS

The nature of the field of mortuary cosmetology, and indeed the field of cosmetology in general, is that earnings grow only as clientele increases. In any aspect of cosmetology, that means low earnings and hard work in the beginning. As cosmetologists develop client loyalty, their earnings will rise. In the mortuary cosmetologist's case, proving the value of one's services to a funeral home or a salon is the key to higher earnings. Mortuary cosmetologists charge more for their services to funeral homes than services in a salon. For example, a haircut and style may cost $20 to $40 in many areas. In the same area, a cut and style done on a visit to a funeral home will bring $40 to $60 because it is a specialized service. However, anyone planning to enter the field should remember it is a relatively new and highly specialized career and demand is still somewhat limited. Mortuary cosmetology is not well known to the general public, and with the higher earnings comes the responsibility of marketing one's services to generate business.

Although specific information on earnings for mortuary cosmetologists is not available, the U.S. Department of Labor does have earning figures for the cosmetology field in general. Median annual earnings in 2005 for salaried hairdressers, hairstylists, and cosmetologists, including tips and commission, were $20,610. Salaries ranged from less than $13,400 to more than $37,380. Earnings are affected by factors such as number of clients, experience, and even location of the business.

WORK ENVIRONMENT

Cosmetic procedures are generally done in a well-ventilated, sterile preparation room. Mortuary cosmetologists generally are not left alone with the deceased; a member of the funeral home staff will generally greet the cosmetologist and be present throughout the services if the cosmetologist desires. Mortuary cosmetologists are not expected to perform cosmetic procedures to a body on a table; rather, the body of the deceased is generally dressed and placed in the casket by the time the mortuary cosmetologist arrives to provide services.

Morticians work all hours. Their work depends basically on a person's time of death. Mortuary cosmetologists, on the other hand, may take an occasional call at an odd hour, but generally perform their services at their earliest convenience. A cosmetologist usually has only a day's notice of services needed at a mortuary, but can perform cosmetic services during day or evening hours, whatever is convenient.

Sanitation is of the utmost importance in funeral homes. Many of the extra steps funeral personnel take in preparation of the body and cleanup of the work area are for sanitary purposes, and mortuary cosmetologists must follow the same standards. Denice Lafferty uses basic equipment provided by the funeral home, such as a hair dryer, curling iron, and combs or brushes. This equipment is used only on the deceased and is thoroughly sterilized in a solution provided by the funeral home. On occasion she has to bring special equipment, such as a small curling iron or a bottle of temporary color. This equipment must be sterilized before she removes it from the funeral home. By the time mortuary cosmetology services are performed, the body has been embalmed, cleaned, and treated with chemical preservatives. Because of these chemicals and for sanitary purposes, mortuary cosmetologists always wear disposable gloves when they are performing cosmetic services.

Some widely held beliefs about bodies of the deceased may concern mortuary cosmetologists, who soon learn that such beliefs are unfounded, or at any rate, have little to do with their services. One commonly held belief is that the hair and nails continue to grow after death. Actually, the skin around the hair follicles and nail cuticles begins to shrink because of dehydration caused by death and the embalming process. Thus the embedded portions of the hair and nails are exposed, giving the impression that they have grown. Another belief—that the deceased move—is not a myth. Rather, it is a rarity that some health care or morgue professionals have witnessed as the body is being handled. Morticians may also notice a rare movement, usually a small twitch, as the body is being prepared with chemicals—generally muscular responses as the chemicals used to preserve tissues are absorbed. The nature of the procedures mortuary cosmetologists perform means that they should not see such movement.

OUTLOOK

Employment for all cosmetologists will grow about as fast as the average for all occupations through 2014, according to the U.S. Department of Labor. The rate of growth for the specialty of mortuary cosmetology is dependent on two factors: how well those in the cosmetology industry market their services and the age of the population and number of deaths. According to statistics compiled by the National Funeral Directors Association, the death rate per thousand in the U.S. population is expected to increase significantly, from 8.82 deaths per thousand in 2000 to 9.9 deaths per thousand in 2030, and 13.17 per thousand in 2060. As the large baby boomer population ages, all careers that provide services to the elderly population are expected to experience steady growth.

FOR MORE INFORMATION

For information on accredited schools, contact
National Accrediting Commission of Cosmetology Arts & Sciences
4401 Ford Avenue, Suite 1300
Alexandria, VA 22302-1432
Tel: 703-600-7600
http://www.naccas.org

For information on membership, contact
National Cosmetology Association
401 North Michigan Avenue, 22nd Floor
Chicago, IL 60611-4267
Tel: 312-527-6765
http://www.ncacares.org

For information on the funeral industry, contact
National Funeral Directors Association
13625 Bishop's Drive
Brookfield, WI 53005-6607
Tel: 800-228-6332
Email: nfda@nfda.org
http://www.nfda.org

Nail Technicians

OVERVIEW

Nail technicians clean, shape, and polish fingernails and toenails. They groom cuticles and apply cream to hands and arms (feet and calves in the case of pedicures). They apply a variety of artificial nails and provide ongoing maintenance. Many nail technicians are skilled in "nail art" and decorate clients' nails with stencils, glitter, and ornaments. Nail technicians may also call themselves *manicurists, pedicurists, nail sculpturists,* or *nail artists.* There are approximately 60,000 nail technicians working in the United States.

HISTORY

The word manicure comes from the Latin *manus* (hand) and *cura* (care). In ancient times, dramatically long and decorated fingernails were a mark of wealth and status, clearly distinguishing an aristocrat from a laborer. Historical artifacts reveal that the practice of caring for and decorating the fingernails dates back thousands of years. The excavation of one Assyrian tomb uncovered a 5,000-year-old cuticle stick. The ancient Egyptians used henna to stain their nails, and cosmetic kits have been discovered even in the tombs of Egyptian women, who took with them everything they might need in the next world.

Makeup remained in fashion throughout the Renaissance, although the Western ideal for fingernails was a natural look. Women took great pains to have soft, beautiful hands. They slept in gloves made from thin leather, lined with almond paste and oil from sperm whales. During this time, the Eastern habit of dyeing the nails and hands continued. Lady Mary Wortley Montague, an upper-class Englishwoman, wrote in 1717 of this practice, "I own I cannot enough accustom my selfe to this fashion to find any Beauty in it." Men and women alike were held to high standards for grooming of the hands during this time, as is evidenced in an 18th-century letter from the Earl of Chesterfield to his son: "Nothing looks more ordinary, vulgar, and illiberal, than dirty hands and ugly, uneven, ragged nails."

The Victorian era frowned upon makeup. Decorative makeup was the mark of a loose woman, so the style for fingernails was au naturel. The end of the 19th century marked the advent of a change in this sentiment, when "nail powders" began to be advertised in Paris. Then, in 1907, liquid nail polish was introduced, the polish lightly tinted with rose dyes. For women who were wary of this new product, solid or powdered nail rouges were available. Nail kits containing files, orange sticks, cuticle implements, and so forth became popular in the first decade of the 20th century. The use of makeup was now becoming acceptable. *Vogue* asserted in 1920, "Even the most conservative and prejudiced people now concede that a woman exquisitely made up may yet be, in spite of seeming frivolity, a faithful wife and devoted mother."

Once the acceptability of makeup was established, a myriad of styles abounded in the 20th century. The year 1930 brought the invention of opaque nail polish as we know it today. Blood-red nails quickly became the rage, although the trendsetting Parisian women were soon sporting green, blue, white, and even black nails to match their clothing ensembles and jewels, sometimes even adding shocking decorative touches not unlike the handiwork of modern-day nail artists.

Also in 1930, *Harper's Bazaar* introduced the idea that fashionable women should match their nail polish and their lipstick. New colors began to flourish in the 1930s, including corals, pinks, and beiges. The 1940s brought yet more naturalistic colors in makeup. In America, Hollywood played a significant role in pushing makeup into the realm of the glamorous. Production of makeup slowed down during World War II as supplies became scarce. But the makeup frenzy exploded in the 1950s when the marketing geniuses at Revlon dictated that colors should change with the season, and women scrambled to get their hands on each new shade as it was introduced. It was also during the 1950s that a dentist in Philadelphia invented sculptured nails, which were quickly embraced and promoted by celebrities such as Cher and Tina Sinatra. Long, fashionable nails were now within the reach of all women.

Elizabeth Taylor's Cleopatra inspired the dramatic, dark-eyed look of the early 1960s, and the eyes continued to dominate the makeup scene into the 1970s, while lips and nails faded into the background. However, by 1972, wild nail colors were once again in full swing, and Revlon introduced a line called "Lady in the Dark," whose 24 shades included variations of green, purple, blue, and black. Of course, with the concurrent advent of the back-to-nature movement in the 1970s, not every woman rushed out to buy the latest shade. A truly natural approach to self-care was also developing, which has been largely synthesized into the concepts and products of the last two decades.

Today, both decorative and natural makeup styles have an established place, and there are fingernail products and styles to suit everyone. While many nail products (including artificial nail kits) continue to be widely available at the retail level, more and more women—and men—are seeking out the services of professional nail technicians.

THE JOB

Nail technicians generally work at a manicurist table and chair or stool across from their clients. Their work implements include finger bowls, electric heaters, wet sanitizer containers, alcohol, nail sticks and files, cuticle instruments, emery boards and buffers, tweezers, nail polishes and removers, abrasives, creams and oils, and nail dryers.

Standard manicure procedure involves removing old polish, shaping nails, softening and trimming cuticles and applying cuticle cream, cleansing and drying hands and nails, applying polish and topcoat, and applying hand lotion. As an extra service, lotion is often massaged into the wrists and arms as well as the hands. Technicians should always follow a sanitary cleanup procedure at their stations following each manicure, including sanitizing instruments and table, discarding used materials, and washing and drying their hands.

A man's manicure is a more conservative procedure than a woman's; the process is similar, but most men prefer to have a dry polish or to have their nails buffed.

Pedicuring has become a popular and important salon service, especially when fashion and weather dictate open-toed shoe styles. The procedure for a pedicure is much like that of a manicure, with the set-up involving a low stool for the technician and an ottoman for the client's feet.

Nail technicians also provide other services, including the application of artificial nails. A number of techniques are employed,

Beauty Firsts

3000 B.C.:   Nail polish

1000 B.C. (or earlier):   Perfume

1878 A.D.:   Vaseline petroleum jelly

1890 A.D.:   Electric hair dryer

1907 A.D.:   Synthetic hair dye

1916 A.D.:   Bobby pins

1923 A.D.:   Cotton swabs

1936 A.D.:   Sunscreen

1965 A.D.:   Antiperspirant aerosol deodorant

Source: About.com

depending on the individual client's preferences and nail character-istics. These include nail wrapping, nail sculpturing, nail tipping, press-on nails, and nail dipping. Technicians also repair broken nails and do "fill-ins" on artificial nails as the real nails grow out.

Nail technicians must take care to use only new or sanitized instruments to prevent the spread of disease. The rapid growth of this industry has been accompanied by an increased awareness of the many ways in which viral, fungal, and bacterial infections can be spread. Many states have passed laws regarding the use of various instruments. Although nail technicians may be exposed to such contagious diseases as athlete's foot and ringworm, the use of gloves is not a practical solution due to the level of precision required in a nail technician's work. For this reason, nail techni-cians must be able to distinguish between skin or nail conditions that can be treated in the salon and disorders and diseases that require medical attention. In so doing, educated and honest nail technicians can contribute to the confidence, health, and well-being of their customers.

REQUIREMENTS
High School
Many states require that nail technicians be high school graduates, although a few states require only an eighth- or 10-grade education. If you are interested in becoming a nail technician, consider taking health and anatomy classes in high school. These classes will give

you a basis for understanding skin and nail conditions. Since many nail technicians are self-employed, you may benefit from taking business classes that teach you how a successful business is run. Take art classes, such as painting, drawing, or sculpting, which will allow you to work with your hands and develop a sense of color and design. Finally, do not forget to take English or communication classes. These courses will help you hone your speaking and writing skills, which you will need when dealing with the public. Some high schools with vocational programs may offer cosmetology courses. Such courses may include the study of bacteriology, sanitation, and mathematics. These specialized courses can be helpful in preparing students for their future work. You will need to check with your high school about the availability of such a vocational program.

Postsecondary Training

Your next step on the road to becoming a nail technician is to attend a cosmetology or nail school. Some states have schools specifically for nail technician training; in other states, the course work must be completed within the context of a full cosmetology program. Nail technology courses generally require between 100 and 500 clock hours of training, but requirements can vary widely from state to state. Because of these variations, make sure the school you choose to attend will allow you to meet the educational requirements of the state in which you hope to work. When the required course work has been completed, the student must pass an examination that usually includes a written test and a practical examination to demonstrate mastery of required skills. A health certificate is sometimes required.

Course work in nail schools (or nail technician programs in cosmetology schools) reflects that students are expected to learn a great deal more than just manicuring; typical courses of study encompass a broad array of subjects. The course outline at Pivot Point International (with affiliated schools throughout the United States) includes bacteriology, sanitation, and aseptic control procedures; diseases and disorders of the nail; anatomy (of the nails, hands, and feet); nail styling and artificial nail techniques; spa manicures and pedicures; aromatherapy; reflexology; state law; advertising and sales; and people skills. Course work also includes working on live models so that each student graduates with hands-on experience in each service studied.

Certification or Licensing

Most states require nail technicians to be licensed. Usually a fee is charged to take the exam, and another fee is assessed before receiving

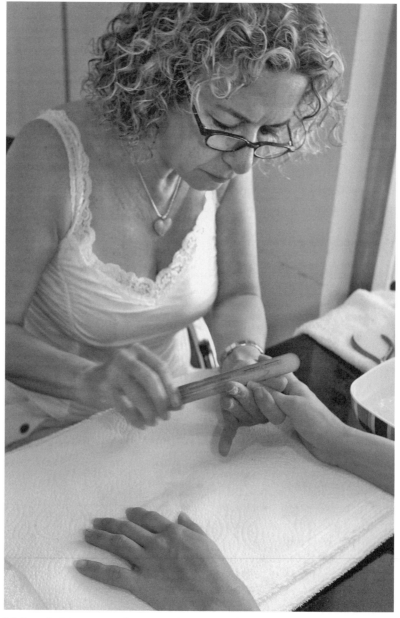

Nail technicians must have good vision and manual dexterity, as their work is very exacting in nature. *(The Image Works)*

the license. Exams usually include both written and practical tests. Many states now offer special nail technician licenses (sometimes called limited or specialty certificates), which require anywhere from

100 to 500 hours of schooling in a licensed cosmetology or nail school. In states where no limited certificates are offered, a student must complete cosmetology school (substantially more hours than required for a specialty), become licensed as a cosmetologist, and then specialize in nail technology. Some states offer special licenses for manicurist managers and nail technician instructors; these require substantially more hours of schooling than do nail technician licenses. Reciprocity agreements exist in some states that enable a nail technician to work in another state without being retested. Some states require that nail technicians be 16 or 18 years old in order to be licensed. You will need to find out the licensing requirements for the state in which you hope to work. Associations and state boards of health can often supply this information.

Other Requirements

Nail technicians must have good vision and manual dexterity, as their work is very exacting in nature. Creativity and artistic talents are helpful, especially in those technicians who perform nail art, which can include painting designs and applying various decorative items to nails. A steady hand is important, and nail technicians should also have an eye for form and color.

Since nail technicians provide services to a wide variety of people, the personality and attitude of a nail technician to a large extent ultimately determine his or her success. While some clients are easy to please, others are demanding and even unreasonable; a nail technician who is able to satisfy even the most difficult customers will be positioned to develop a large, loyal following. Nail technicians who are punctual, courteous, respectful, and patient will enjoy a distinct competitive advantage over others in the industry that lack these qualities. Tact, professionalism, and competence are important. Knowledge and practice of proper sanitizing techniques should be clearly visible to clients. Naturally, hygiene and grooming are of paramount importance in this profession, and a nail technician's own hands and nails should be perfectly groomed; this is one's best form of advertisement and can help foster confidence in prospective and new clients.

A confident, outgoing personality can be a great boon to a nail technician's success. Customers may readily accept recommendations for additional nail services from a persuasive, knowledgeable, and competent nail technician who appears genuinely interested in the customer's interests. Nail technicians who can successfully sell their services will enjoy increased business.

Unlike most careers in the cosmetology field, nail technicians are not required to be on their feet all day. Nail technology is a good choice for those interested in the beauty industry who prefer to be able to work in a seated, comfortable position.

EXPLORING

If you are considering a career as a nail technician, a good avenue of exploration is to call a cosmetology or nail school and ask for an opportunity to tour the facilities, observe classes, and question instructors. Another enjoyable option is for you to make an appointment with a nail technician for a manicure or pedicure. By receiving one of these services yourself, you will have the opportunity to visit the place of business, take in the atmosphere, and experience the procedure. In addition, you'll have the opportunity to talk to someone who can answer your questions about this line of work. Explain that you are interested in becoming a nail technician, and you may find that you can develop a mentoring relationship with this professional technician. A part-time job in a beauty salon that offers nail services may also help you determine your interest in various aspects of the beauty industry. Part-time positions for nontechnicians in nail salons, though, may prove difficult to find.

EMPLOYERS

As with cosmetologists and other personal appearance workers, approximately half of the nail technicians in the country are self-employed. They may rent a "booth" or chair at a salon; some may own their own nail salons. A growing number of nail technicians are employed by nail salons, which are rapidly increasing in number in many areas of the country. Beauty shops and department store salons also employ nail technicians, but most have only one or two on staff (very large salons have more). Since nail services represent one of the fastest-growing segments of the cosmetology industry, there is good potential for those wishing to open their own businesses in the nail industry.

STARTING OUT

In most states, graduating from an accredited cosmetology or nail school that meets the state's requirements for licensing is the vehicle for entry into this field. Nearly all cosmetology schools assist graduates with the process of finding employment. Want ads and personal visits to salons and shops are also productive means of finding a job.

ADVANCEMENT

Advancement in the nail technology industry most often takes the form of establishing a large, loyal clientele. Other opportunities include owning one's own nail salon. This can be a highly profitable endeavor if one has the proper business skills and savvy; the cost of materials and overhead can be relatively low, and, in addition to the earnings realized from services performed for their customers, the owners typically receive half of their operators' earnings.

Some technicians choose to advance by becoming nail instructors in cosmetology or nail schools or becoming inspectors for state cosmetology boards.

Nail technicians who constantly strive to increase their knowledge and proficiency in a wide array of nail services will have a competitive advantage and will be positioned to secure a large and varied clientele.

EARNINGS

Income for nail technicians can vary widely, depending on the skill, experience, and clientele of the nail technician, the type and location of the shop or salon, the tipping habits of the clientele, and the area of the country. The U.S. Department of Labor reports the median annual income for manicurists was $18,280 in 2005. (This income includes tips.) The lowest paid 10 percent earned $13,640 or less while the highest paid 10 percent earned $30,820 or more. Those working in large metropolitan areas may have slightly higher earnings, but the cost of living is also higher there. According to findings by *NAILS Magazine*, which surveyed professionals to come up with 2005 statistics on the industry, nail technicians serviced on average about 36 clients per week and charged on average approximately $17 for a manicure. Given these figures, a technician who works 50 weeks a year (with two weeks off for vacation) would earn $30,600. Advanced Cosmetology Educational Services reports the cost of a booth rental varied between regions and from salon to salon, ranging from $75 per week up to $150 per week, or $300 to $600 per month with an average of $5,500 per year. Deducting this charge from the technician's earnings leaves the technician with a base income of approximately $25,100. Obviously, tips have not been figured into this income, and they may raise earnings by several thousand dollars per year.

The importance of the talents and personality of the nail technician cannot be underestimated when evaluating potential earnings. Those who hold themselves to the highest levels of professionalism, express a genuine interest in clients' well-being, and provide the highest quality service quickly develop loyal clienteles, and these nail technicians will realize earnings that far exceed the averages.

Those technicians who work in beauty shops are less likely than those in nail salons to have appointments scheduled throughout the day; however, customers in beauty salons often pay more and tip better for these services. Also, there is less competition within the beauty shop setting, as the majority of beauty salons employ only one or two nail technicians.

Owning one's own nail salon can be very profitable, as the cost of equipment is relatively low. In addition to taking home one's own earnings from servicing clients, the owner also generally gets half of the income generated by the shop's other operators. Nail salons are a prime example of a small business with tremendous potential for success.

Except for those nail technicians who work in department stores or large salons, most do not enjoy much in the way of benefits; few nail technicians receive health and life insurance or paid vacations.

WORK ENVIRONMENT

Nail technicians work indoors in bright, well-ventilated, comfortable environments. Unlike most careers in the cosmetology industry that require operators to be on their feet most of the day, nail technicians perform their work seated at a table.

Many nail technicians work five-day weeks including Saturdays, which are a high-volume business day in this industry. Working some evenings may be helpful in building one's clientele, as a large percentage of customers are working professionals. Nail technicians often enjoy some flexibility in their hours, and many enjoy successful part-time careers.

A large number of nail technicians are self-employed; they may rent a space in a beauty or nail salon. Often, nail technicians must provide their own supplies and tools. Nail technicians are exposed to a certain amount of chemicals and dust, but this is generally manageable in well-ventilated work surroundings. Those who work in full-service salons may be exposed to additional chemicals and odors.

Inherent in the nature of a nail technician's work is the constant company of others. A nail technician who is not a people person will find this line of work most challenging. But since most people who choose this career enjoy the company of others, they find the opportunity to talk with and get to know people to be one of the most satisfying and enjoyable aspects of their work.

OUTLOOK

The nail business (a multibillion dollar industry) has been growing rapidly for years. Nail salons and day spas offering nail services continue to crop up everywhere, and nail technicians represent the fastest-growing segment of the various specialized service providers in the beauty industry. According to the U.S. Department of Labor, employment for nail technicians should grow faster than the average for all occupations through 2014.

Once a mark of feminine status, nail services are now sought and enjoyed by a wide variety of people, both male and female. Helen Barkan, whose clients have dubbed her the "Nail Doctor," has been a nail technician and salon owner in the Deerbrook Mall in Deerfield, Illinois, for the past 24 years, and she has been doing nails for more years than she'll reveal. Barkan, whose straightforward services focus on helping clients grow strong, healthy nails (she doesn't do artificial nails), says, "Many of my clients have been coming to me for more than 20 years. I've always been willing to spend a little extra time and go the extra mile for my customers, and at one time I worked seven days a week. My clients are important to me, and they know that." Barkan has watched the industry change dramatically over the decades. Today, approximately one-third of Barkan's customers are men, and they come for manicures and pedicures alike. Clearly, there is a market for all kinds of nail services, from the most basic hand and nail care to the most involved procedures and outlandish styles.

FOR MORE INFORMATION

This magazine has information on the latest nail technologies, fashions, safety issues, and industry news.
NAILS Magazine
3520 Challenger Street
Torrance, CA 90503-1640
Tel: 310-533-2400
http://www.nailsmag.com

This organization accredits cosmetology schools nationally and can provide lists of licensed training schools.
National Accrediting Commission of Cosmetology Arts and Sciences
4401 Ford Avenue, Suite 1300
Alexandria, VA 22302-1432
Tel: 703-600-7600
http://www.naccas.org

This organization of nail technicians, stylists, salon owners, and other professionals can provide industry and education information.

National Cosmetology Association
401 North Michigan Avenue, 22nd Floor
Chicago, IL 60611-4267
Tel: 312-527-6765
http://www.salonprofessionals.org

This Web site for beauty professionals has a list of state licensing requirements for nail technicians.

Beauty Tech
http://www.beautytech.com/nailtech

Salon Managers

OVERVIEW

Salon managers may occupy positions in beauty salons, day spas, children's salons, nursing homes, and cruise lines. Their primary duties are to maintain a congenial rapport between clients and personnel, oversee the financial budget, manage inventory, and supervise employees. Salon managers must be personable, able to withstand the pressures of a rigorous day, and dressed for success since their appearance can act as an advertisement for their salon. The manager is often responsible for hiring employees, policing their licenses, enforcing health and sanitary conditions, and maintaining accurate records. Each state stipulates its requirements for salons; in Washington, D.C., the Cosmetology Act states, "Every Beauty Salon shall have a manager, who shall have immediate charge and supervision over the operators practicing cosmetology."

HISTORY

The origin of beauty culture began in ancient times, when an attractive appearance was associated with physical well-being. Personal embellishments, such as kohl, a form of eye shadow, were used by the Egyptians, Sumerians, Hebrews, and Babylonians to adorn the dead, dress for political ceremony, and enhance individual grooming. The science of cosmetics continued beyond the fall of the Roman Empire, into the Renaissance, and finally to modern day use. In 1914, cosmetic sales totaled $39.8 million and grew to $449.9 million in 1940; they climbed to $32 billion in 2005, and are still expanding.

The origin of barbers also predates modern times. The Egyptian papyri (written papers) refer to barbers as conveyors of news and advice, and barbershops became a favorite meeting place. Early Christian monasteries bestowed on barbers the honor of shaving the hair of monks. In the Middle Ages, barbers treated medical illnesses, cauterizing wounds, treating abscesses, and extracting teeth. Barbers were referred to as "doctors of the short robe," while academically trained doctors were known as "doctors of the long robe." Barbers' knowledge of human anatomy and physiology combined with the cosmetic applications of cremes, oils, and hair colorings to create the beauty culture of modern day. The profession enhanced the creative and artistic talents of the cosmeticians, while it grew in tandem with the fashion world.

Hairstyling salons, which were once patronized only by the privileged class, have become commonplace. Today approximately 670,000 licensed cosmetologists work in the United States. As women continue to enter the business world and the pace of society quickens, time-efficient salons and salons/spas are in demand. New techniques in skin care, hair conditioning, and nail sculpture continue to add to the industry's popularity. Day spas have cropped up everywhere to offer total makeovers. Beauty enhancing treatments, such as skin exfoliation, scalp massages, and pedicures with tension-busting acupressure, are familiar procedures in the relaxing environments of the beauty industry.

A good example of the growing salon industry is the Minneapolis-based cosmetics firm Aveda, now in business for over 20 years. The company has developed a million-dollar business, offering numerous products available in stores across the United States and other countries such as Canada, Germany, Indonesia, Iceland, and Italy. "Aveda is on the cutting edge when it comes to natural products," says David Vladyak, project manager with Kline and Company, a cosmetic market research firm.

Because cosmetologists have become absorbed in providing these many different services, they have little or no time to spend in management. This situation has created a need for efficient salon managers to free cosmetologists from routine business tasks.

THE JOB

A salon manager's responsibilities include business administration, public relations, and personnel management. Most crucial to success, however, is a wonderful personality and a positive mental outlook. "A good manager should always be upbeat and happy, and be a pleasant person at all times. It doesn't matter what is going

A salon manager schedules an appointment with a customer. *(The Image Works)*

on in your personal life," says Andrea Blackshaw, co-owner of The Scissor's Edge, a unisex hair salon in Winnetka, Illinois.

All salons should have financial budgets to allocate funds and good bookkeeping systems. Managers should maintain records of daily, weekly, and yearly expenses, as well as files on each patron. Managers must check to see if the dates of the operators' licenses are current. They should be familiar with insurance policies for fire, theft, and health, be on good terms with the salon's accountants and lawyers, and review the regulations established by the state board of cosmetology.

A large portion of the manager's job is based on the psychology of communication. The manager should be a good liaison between operators and clients and be readily available to handle complaints and adjustments with minimal fuss. The manager's role is to build good will; therefore, he or she should become acquainted with the different people who enter the salon. Verbal skills are important, and managers should instruct their receptionists on proper telephone etiquette; a receptionist with a pleasant tone and gentle mood invites the customer to return.

The salon's decor is often another managerial concern, and some managers function as design consultants as well. Arranging an attractive cosmetic display and keeping a spotless salon are also important considerations when creating a welcoming environment.

Safety is a concern, too, so every salon manager must have access to a first-aid kit, and an emergency telephone number, and should be familiar with CPR.

Delaware, Maryland, Minnesota, North Dakota, Ohio, and South Dakota have separate laws for cosmeticians who are also managers; they are called manager-operators. Minnesota and Ohio require specific licenses for cosmetologists who only want to be a manicurist-manager. Manager-operators are often interim positions between doing cosmetology work and owning one's own business. Manager-operators must be licensed as cosmetologists within their state; they are paid a percentage of the salon's profits; and, unlike managers who are not operators, they are allowed to style hair. They also have the advantage of prior experience and are already familiar with various aspects of the business.

REQUIREMENTS

High School

Does working as a salon manager sound interesting to you? There are a number of courses you can take in high school to help prepare you for this career. Classes in health, anatomy, and chemistry will give you a science background that will be helpful both in your postsecondary education and your career when you will deal with sanitation issues, chemical products, and new procedures. Since managing finances will be in your future, take business, accounting, and mathematics classes. Computer classes that teach you how to work with spreadsheet programs will also be beneficial. Psychology classes may provide you with a basis for understanding people, which will be an asset when you work with a variety of customers and employees. Finally, take any studio art courses that you can. Painting, sculpting, or photography, for example, will give you the opportunity to develop your sense of color and design, important qualities for anyone working in the beauty industry.

Some high schools offer vocational programs in cosmetology, and some cosmetology schools allow high school students to begin their studies there as they also work to complete high school. In both of these specialized programs, students typically study such topics as sanitation procedures, sciences, mathematics, and even legal issues of the industry.

Postsecondary Training

Although a few salon managers may only have a business background, the majority of salon managers have risen to this position by first working as a cosmetologist, barber-stylist, or manager-operator. To become a cosmetologist or barber, plan on attending an accredited cosmetology or barber school. Full-time programs vary in length but generally last from 10 to 24 months. Work will include classroom study and hands-on experiences. You will study such topics as chemistry, hygiene, anatomy, and proper care of your tools and equipment. In addition, a good program will also cover general business practices and legal issues. The National Accrediting Commission of Cosmetology Arts and Sciences (NAC-CAS) can provide you with a listing of accredited schools across the country. (The organization's contact information is given at the end of this article.) All states require barbers and cosmetologists to be licensed, but the requirements vary from state to state. It is important, therefore, that you find out what your state requires and make sure the program you are interested in will allow you to meet those requirements. Because the manager-operator position allows a professional to gain business and management experience, those who have worked in this position are often the best prepared to become full-time salon managers.

Certification or Licensing

There is no certification or licensing for salon managers, per se, nor are there labor unions. However, a salon manager who is also a cosmetologist, barber, or manager-operator must be licensed. To receive a license you will need to pass a state exam, which is generally a written test but may also include a demonstration and an oral test. As noted above, requirements for licensing vary by state; therefore, you will need to determine the requirements for the state in which you hope to practice before you begin your education. Students who have passed their state test and applied for a license are issued temporary permits in most states. Temporary permits allow them to practice their profession while they wait to receive the actual license.

Even after a cosmetologist or barber has become licensed their education must continue. Many states require them to take a specified number of credit hours, called continuing-education units or CEUs, to keep their licenses current. Again, these requirements vary by state; state licensing boards will have complete information.

Other Requirements

Hair styles change from season to season. New techniques are continuously being developed for working with hair, nails, and skin. Customers' expectations of their salon experience also change with the times. Because the salon manager works in this dynamic environment, he or she should enjoy learning about new fashions and figuring out ways to provide new services to customers. The salon manager also needs to have an artistic sense or strong sense of personal style. The manager's looks are an advertisement for the salon; few customers will feel comfortable patronizing a salon where the manager has a bad dye job or ragged nails. And, naturally, the successful salon manager enjoys working with people. "Running a salon is like being a parent in the home," says Terri Ross, hairstylist and owner of J. Terri Ross in Glencoe, Illinois. "A manager solves problems, monitors clients, and takes care of the various personalities that enter. He should be open-minded, assertive, and stick to his guns in dealing with people. The best personality traits he can have are to be optimistic, even tempered, hard-working, and go with the flow."

EXPLORING

Although you won't be able to experience the position of salon manager itself until you are qualified for this work, there are a number of steps you can take to explore this career. Contact a local cosmetology school and request a tour of the facilities. In addition, ask if you can sit in on a class or talk to the instructors and students. This will give you a sense of what the education is like and allow you to talk to others interested in the industry. Also, contact a local salon to arrange for an informational interview either with the salon manager or a cosmetologist. At an informational interview you can ask such questions as: What is the most enjoyable aspect of your job? What is the least enjoyable? What educational route did you take to enter this field? What recommendations do you have for someone interested in the field? If the salon manager is receptive to the idea, you might be able to shadow him or her for a day to see what the typical business day is like. Also, read salon industry magazines, such as *Salon Today*, to find out what issues are important to those working in the field.

Consider gaining some business or management experience. Get a part-time or summer job in a salon or retail business in which you will have to work with customers and develop your people skills. Also, consider joining school clubs or organizations that allow you management roles on projects or give you the opportunity to work with finances, perhaps by balancing the books or acting as treasurer.

Finally, try volunteering at a nursing home or hospital. In these environments you may be in a position to provide personal care services such as washing and styling a patient's hair. Any volunteer work in which you interact with people will also help you hone your communication skills.

EMPLOYERS

Salon managers work in beauty salons, barber shops, children's salons, and nursing homes. They may also work at resorts, spas, and hotels, or for cruise lines. Generally there are more employment opportunities in large cities, which have a greater number of salons, day spas, and other such businesses.

STARTING OUT

Generally, a management position is not considered entry level. Those hoping to become salon managers typically start out as cosmetologists or other stylists after graduating from cosmetology or barber school. These schools provide the opportunity for networking with others in the profession, which may lead to a job, and some may also have placement services for their graduates. Also, industry magazines, Web sites, and local newspapers frequently publish job openings. Trade shows and organization conferences may also provide the opportunity to network for jobs.

ADVANCEMENT

Advancement to the position of salon manager comes through continuing education in the cosmetology field, networking with other professionals, and gaining business experience. Salon managers advance by moving to larger salons where they oversee more employees and have a larger client base. Some managers work toward owning their own salons. Other avenues for advancement include moving into advertising or working in sales in the beauty industry. Success for any manager is largely based on self-motivation, continuous learning, and the ability to interact well with people.

EARNINGS

Although the U.S. Department of Labor does not provide specific salary information for salon managers, it does report earnings for supervisors/managers of retail workers. In 2005, these professionals had median annual earnings of $32,840. The lowest paid 10 percent of this group earned approximately $20,500, while the highest paid 10 percent made approximately $57,420 annually. Generally, a salon manager's income will fall within this range. Salaries for salon managers will also depend on such factors as the location and size of the salon, the clientele, the services provided there, and the manager's experience. Depending on the salon, managers can earn a fixed salary or receive a percentage of the salon's profits. Fringe benefits, health and dental insurance, and paid vacation time are negotiated independently with each salon owner.

WORK ENVIRONMENT

Much of managers' time is spent indoors establishing and maintaining relationships, and they should have a designated area or specific office space in which to confer with employees. They should be easily accessible to the public and still reach the far corners of the salon with ease. Since their presence is always known, they should look their best at all times—not always an easy task for busy directors who put in the longest hours.

The well-designed salon has a pleasing color scheme, an excellent floor plan, and possibly soothing music playing in the background and refreshments available for customers. It is part of the manager's responsibility to ensure a pleasant and sanitary atmosphere. While managers may receive some enjoyment from working in these surroundings, their jobs can also be quite hectic as they balance schedules, cover for sick employees, deal with demanding customers, or order supplies.

OUTLOOK

The U.S. Department of Labor predicts that employment for barbers, cosmetologists, and other workers in the industry will grow about as fast as the average for all occupations through 2014. As long as the beauty industry continues its steady growth there will be opportunities for managers of salons. A major part of the beauty industry's success is due to the growing aging population and its desire to remain youthful.

FOR MORE INFORMATION

Contact this organization for industry news, a listing of accredited schools, and information on financial aid.

National Accrediting Commission of Cosmetology Arts and Sciences
4401 Ford Avenue, Suite 1300
Alexandria, VA 22302-1432
Tel: 703-600-7600
http://www.naccas.org

This organization provides education and networking opportunities for its members.
Professional Beauty Federation, Salon/Spa Section
15825 North 71st Street, Suite 100
Scottsdale, AZ 85254-2187
Tel: 800-468-2274
Email: info@probeauty.org
http://www.probeauty.org/salonspa

For subscription information, contact
Salon Today
Vance Publishing Corporation
400 Knightsbridge Parkway
Lincolnshire, IL 60069-3613
Tel: 847-634-2600
Email: info@vancepublishing.com
http://www.salontoday.com

This Web site provides a listing of schools by state.
BeautySchool.com
http://www.beautyschool.com

For hair styling tips and techniques, job listings, and business advice, visit the following Web site:
BehindtheChair
http://www.behindthechair.com

Spa Attendants

OVERVIEW

Spa attendants work in hotels, resorts, and salons. They are specially trained in facial, body, and water treatments. They assist massage therapists and estheticians and prepare and clean the treatment rooms and tables. They provide spa customers with refreshments, towels, washcloths, and robes. According to the International SPA Association, there are 267,400 people employed by the more than 13,700 spas in the United States.

HISTORY

Fossils prove that even the mammoths of over 20,000 years ago enjoyed a good spa treatment. The town of Hot Springs, a small resort village nestled in the hills of South Dakota, features a fossil excavation site. This site serves as evidence that mammoths were attracted to the area's pools of warm water. Humans share this attraction. Native Americans considered natural hot springs to be sacred healing grounds. Throughout Europe, the ancient Romans built colossal spas, including the Baths of Caracalla, one of the Seven Wonders of the World. Only its ruins remain, but these baths once featured hot and cold baths, a swimming pool, a gymnasium, shops, art galleries, and acres of gardens.

Although spas fell out of favor during the Middle Ages, by the 17th and 18th centuries they had once again become popular in Europe. An interest in making use of natural resources for healing and relaxation spread. By the late 1800s there was hardly a well of natural spring water in the United States that a businessman had not capitalized upon. At the turn of the century in the United States, people visited resorts and spas (with or without natural hot springs) for exercise and relaxation. By the 1920s spas had become popular retreats for the wealthy. Since that time, spas have diversified their services and attracted a wide range of visitors. Today's spas have clients ranging from busy professionals looking for several hours of stress reduction, to families looking for healthy vacations, to pregnant women seeking relaxation, to men looking to keep fit. According to the International SPA Association, there were 131 million spa visits in the United States in 2005.

THE JOB

From the ylang-ylang plant to the *lomilomi* massage, a new language of health and rejuvenation has emerged in recents years. Although there were only 30 spas in the United States in the late 1970s, the number now has grown past 13,700. Nearly 11,000 of these are day spas, where clients can check in for an afternoon of relaxation and rejuvenation. The remainder are resort/hotel spas, medical spas, club spas, and destination spas, which welcome clients for longer visits. Spas and resorts have cropped up around natural hot springs, the seaside, the desert, the mountains, and even the plains. Some spas are designed to meet very specific needs, such as weight management and holistic wellness. While most spas offer the usual facials, body wraps, and massages, many are expanding to include "mind/body awareness" as people flock to spas for both physical and spiritual needs. In some spas, you can schedule hypnosis, yoga, and dream therapy sessions right after your horseback riding, tennis game, and round of golf. So the duties of a spa attendant can vary greatly from location to location. Spa attendants are also finding work outside of the vacation industry, at salons and day spas, as cosmetologists recognize the need to expand into other areas of beauty care. In addition to actually performing treatments, spa attendants devise special treatment plans for individual clients. They also schedule appointments, order and sell products, launder linens, and clean all spa areas. They offer advice on treatments and skin care products.

Craig Rabago works as a men's spa technician for the Ihilani Resort and Spa in Kapolei, Hawaii. *Ihilani* means "heavenly splendor," and it is part of Rabago's job to help guests realize this splendor. "I create an atmosphere that is heavenly for them," Rabago explains. "I'm of Hawaiian descent and a local. I give people a warm welcome and make them feel at home." Rabago has been trained in a variety of services, including seaweed wraps, salt scrubs, and *thalasso* hydrotherapy (a fresh seawater massage). The Ihilani features a fitness center and separate spas for men and women; each spa includes a sauna, steam room, needle shower, hot tub, and cold plunge. For the popular "cool ti leaf wrap," Rabago prepares a table in one of the spa's private rooms, spreading out the long, frond-like Hawaiian ti leaves and treating them with special oils. When the guest arrives for his wrap, Rabago gives him a robe and sandals and shows him to the lockers and showers. When the guest is ready for the treatment, Rabago then brings him to the treatment room

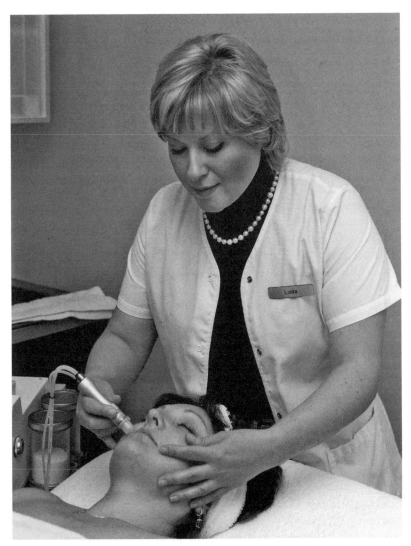

A spa attendant gives a facial to a client. *(The Image Works)*

and directs him to lie back on the table. As he explains the treatment, Rabago rubs the guest's skin with oils and lotions, making sure to pay special attention to sunburn, dry skin, and other trouble areas. He then wraps the guest in a damp sheet. Rabago leaves him wrapped for 25 minutes, checking in occasionally to make sure the guest is comfortable. In between treatments, Rabago must take linen inventory and keep the spa areas clean. He also does a fair amount of work on the computer. "But taking care of the guests' needs—that's my priority," Rabago says.

The Ihilani capitalizes on its locale, providing treatments with fresh seawater, sea salt, seaweed, and Hawaiian plants. In a different kind of environment, a spa and resort may provide very different services. Mud baths, natural hot spring whirlpools, volcanic mineral treatment—resort owners around the world develop their spas with the natural surroundings in mind. This results in very specific training for spa attendants. "The training was time-consuming," Rabago recalls. "The spa techs train with each other. We put in lots of hours of practice before we actually go to work on a guest."

High School

To prepare for work as a spa attendant, take high school courses in anatomy, physiology, and biology. These classes will give you an understanding of the human body and muscle systems. Chemistry will prepare you for the use and preparation of skin care products. Health courses will teach you about nutrition, fitness, and other issues of importance to the health-conscious patrons of resorts and spas. Because so many spas offer treatment for both the body and the mind, take some psychology courses to learn about the history of treating depression, anxiety, and other mental and emotional problems. Finally, take computer classes, which will allow you to become comfortable using this technology. If in your future job you need to keep track of spa supplies, you will probably be using a computer to do so.

In addition to these classes, you will benefit from having CPR and first aid training. Check with your high school to find out if it offers such training or contact organizations such as your local Red Cross. Many spas require attendants to know CPR and first aid, and your training will give you an advantage when looking for a job.

Postsecondary Training

Currently no specific postsecondary training program exists for spa attendants. Most spas put new hires through their own attendant training programs. Any work experience that you already have in a spa, therefore, will make you an appealing job candidate. During your high school years, try to get a summer job at one of the many resorts across the country. Spas often hire extra help to deal with the increased number of guests during this peak vacation period. Although you may only be working with the laundry, you will have the opportunity to see how a spa or resort is run and find out about the many different jobs available.

Some spas require their attendants to be certified cosmeticians or massage therapists. In such cases, education beyond high school is required. If you know of a specific spa at which you wish to work, ask about the hiring policy for attendants. Cosmeticians receive their training from cosmetology schools; massage therapists are educated at schools of massage therapy. Licensing requirements for these professionals vary by state, and you should know what these requirements are before you begin a program of study.

Other Requirements

Craig Rabago advises that a good spa attendant should be happy, courageous, and ambitious. Guests of resorts and spas expect to be pampered and welcomed and can only fully relax during a spa treatment if the attendant is calm and considerate. Be prepared to serve your clients and to remain friendly and helpful. "But don't be timid and shy," Rabago says. "This is a good way to meet people from all around the world. You can broaden your horizons."

Any shyness and excessive modesty may also prevent you from performing your spa duties properly. You'll be applying lotions and oils to the naked skin of your guests—if you are uncomfortable, your clients will detect it and become uncomfortable themselves. You must take a professional approach so that your clients feel safe and at ease. You should have a good "bedside manner"—the calm, comforting approach health care professionals use. Self-confidence is also important; you must convey to your client that you're knowledgeable about the treatment.

EXPLORING

One of the best ways to explore this type of work is to get a part-time or summer job at a spa. You may be surprised by the number of spas in your area. There may even be a resort on the outskirts of your city. Do an Internet search for "Beauty Salons and Services" as well as "Health Clubs" and "Massage" in your area. Visit a salon or day spa and ask to interview someone who works as a spa attendant. Some attendants may allow you to shadow them for a day or two. Larger salons may have openings for part-time attendants, allowing you to gather firsthand experience.

Many resorts across the country advertise nationally for summer help. Check the classified advertisments of vacation and travel magazines, and visit http://www.resortjobs.com for a listing. You could also select a resort and spa from the pages of tourism publications, such as *Resorts and Great Hotels* (http://www.resortsgreathotels.com), and call the hotel directly to request information about summer jobs. *Spa Finder* (http://www.spafinder.com) magazine also publishes a directory of spas.

If you are unable to find a job at a spa, consider a part-time or summer job at a local hotel, beauty salon, or tanning salon. In any of these locations you will gain experience working with guests and providing for their comfort. Nursing homes and hospitals also employ high school students to provide clients or patients with personal care services. Working at a retail store specializing in products for skin care and beauty, aromatherapy, and massage can teach you about various spa treatments and products and help you decide if you are interested in this line of work.

If you have the money, consider making an appointment for yourself at a spa in your area. You may not be able to afford a vacation or full-day treatment, but even an hour spent as a client at a spa can give you an impression of what working in such an environment would be like.

EMPLOYERS

The International SPA Association estimates that, as of 2006, 267,400 people worked in the spa industry in the United States, an increase of 52,000 workers since 2004. Spas have grown at a very rapid rate over the past decade, and they should continue to do so as more people begin to value the benefits of spa visits. The primary employers of spa attendants are hotels, resorts, salons, and, naturally, spas. Increasing numbers of salons are adding spas to their facilities to maintain a competitive edge; this will lead to increased opportunities for spa attendants throughout the country, mostly in larger cities and metropolitan areas. The same is true for hotel spas. Many spas, however, are clustered in resort areas with attractions like hot springs and consistently pleasant climates.

STARTING OUT

Many spa attendants receive their training on the job, but some background experience in health care or cosmetology may help you in landing that first job as a spa attendant. Craig Rabago, for example, worked as a surgical aide before going to work for the Ihilani. "The work is related," he said, "but it's a very different atmosphere." He learned about the spa job from a listing in the newspaper. If you are not particular about your geographic location, check travel publications for listings of resorts and spas, or visit http://www.spafinder.com on the Web, and contact the spas about job openings. *Spa Finder*, both online and in their print directory, lists spas according to their specialties and locations.

A degree from a cosmetology or massage therapy school can be valuable when looking for a job in a spa. Many of these degree programs require fieldwork, or hands-on experience, and will put you in touch with salons and fitness centers. Without a degree, you may be limited in the spa treatments you are allowed to perform. But as more and more individual hairstylists and beauty salons open day spas to accommodate all the needs of their clients, both licensed and unlicensed spa attendants will find more job opportunities.

ADVANCEMENT

The longer an attendant works in a spa, the more he or she will learn about the services provided there. The attendant will also have more opportunities to expand upon the on-the-job training and potentially be allowed to perform more treatments. Though attendants typically start off with only an hourly wage, they can eventually receive commissions and tips. The more guests an attendant works with, the better tips and commission he or she will make. In a salon or day spa situation, the clientele will include regular customers. If they are happy with an attendant's work, they will request that attendant's services specifically and thus increase the attendant's income.

Attendants who complete further formal education also become qualified for more advanced positions. Those who attend cosmetology school to become *cosmeticians* typically take classes such as anatomy, chemistry, and physiology. They are qualified to work on the skin, giving facials, body wraps, and makeup applications, and may also do hair removal by waxing or plucking. Nail technician programs offered through cosmetology schools or nail schools qualify the graduate to give manicures and pedicures. Attendants who are particularly interested in fitness may want to consider advancement by getting an associate's degree from a fitness program. Courses for such programs include muscle conditioning, nutrition, and injury prevention. Those interested in massage may seek advancement by completing a massage therapy school program, which will qualify them to give different types of massage. These programs include course work in anatomy and physiology as well as provide hands-on training.

Some attendants advance to become *spa program directors*. As program directors, they are responsible for adding new services, training spa attendants, determining what skin products to use, and controlling other details of the spa's daily practices. Those who wish to run their own business may eventually open their own spa.

EARNINGS

Salaries for spa attendants vary greatly across the country, so no significant salary survey has been conducted in recent years. Spa attendants make from minimum wage to around $10 per hour. Salaries vary according to work environment (a large resort will pay more than a small salon) and the spa attendant's responsibilities. Spa attendants are either paid by the hour or by commission (a percentage of the spa treatments performed). Spa attendants also receive tips of between 10 and 15 percent. Some spas automatically bill guests an additional percentage to cover the tip, so that the guest doesn't have to worry about having the money on hand to give to the attendant. With tips from a wealthy clientele and a commission on higher-priced services, a spa attendant at a fine hotel will make much more than an attendant in a smaller day spa. Employees of spas are likely to receive better benefits than many of their counterparts in the cosmetology field. Spa attendants working at hotels may also receive a variety of perks, such as discounted spa treatments, guest rooms, meals in the hotel restaurants, and travel packages.

Spa Facts

- The spa industry generated over $9.7 billion in revenues in 2005.
- There were 131 million spa visits in 2005.
- Approximately 267,400 people were employed in the spa industry in 2006.
- There were 13,757 spas in the United States in 2006.
- In 2006, the northeastern United States had the most spas (3,131); the northwestern United States had the fewest (764).
- Nearly 80 percent of spas in 2006 were day spas. Resort/hotel spas made up 9 percent of all spas; medical spas, 7 percent; club spas, 4 percent; mineral springs spas, 0.6 percent; and destination spas, 0.5 percent.

Source: International SPA Association

WORK ENVIRONMENT

Working among vacationers in a sunny, scenic part of the world can be very enjoyable. Most spa attendants work within well-decorated, temperature-controlled buildings, with soothing music piped through the speaker systems. Fresh fruit, tea, and other refreshments are often readily available. Spa attendants work directly with a public that has come to a resort to alleviate stress and other worries, making for very relaxed interactions. Some hotel spa attendants even live on the premises in special employee quarters, or in nearby housing, allowing them to live close to the beaches, mountains, or whatever natural beauty surrounds the resort.

Because spas usually open in the wee hours of the morning and close after dark, spa attendants may have to work long, irregular hours. Depending on the codes of the spa, they wear uniforms and jackets. They also wear gloves if their skin is sensitive to some of the products.

In a local beauty salon, a spa attendant tries to maintain a similarly relaxed environment in the few rooms dedicated to spa treatment. The rest of the salon, however, may be noisy with waiting customers, hair dryers, electric clippers, and music. The salon may also affect those with allergies to chemicals in hair treatment products.

Day spas, which may be located in large cities, typically strive to maintain a serene environment for the clientele, from the reception area, where soft music may be playing in the background, to the private treatment rooms, which may have soft lighting. While the spa attendant may work in these areas, he or she is also part of the activity behind the scenes, often working with damp laundry, cleaning supplies, and spa products.

OUTLOOK

The International SPA Association reports that spa visits are on the rise in the United States, with clients making 131 million spa visits in 2005 alone. This increase can be attributed to the growing appreciation for the benefits of spa visits, the increased number of day spas, and increased popularity of spas among men. In fact, many spas are adding treatments specifically for men. These expanding facilities and new treatment options should translate into job opportunities for everyone working in this industry, including spa attendants.

In addition, the public is becoming more health conscious, and people are looking to spas for both enjoyable and educational vacations. Some spas are specializing in teaching guests new patterns of diet, exercise, and skin care. A number of health care professionals are even predicting that spas will be covered by health insurance plans; doctors will write prescriptions to patients for spa treatments. To compete with other spas, and to satisfy returning guests, spas are likely to offer even more diverse lists of services and treatments. The spa attendant will have to keep ahead of health and beauty trends and be capable of adapting to new programs and methods.

Anticipating a future of one-stop beauty treatment, the owners of hair and beauty salons are dedicating rooms to spa treatments. For the cost of a little remodeling, hair salons can stay competitive with local day spas, as well as generate more business. Spa attendants may find their best job opportunities at these salons, where they can earn a good commission and establish a client base.

FOR MORE INFORMATION

For employment opportunities, contact
Day Spa Association
310 17th Street
Union City, NJ 07087-4310
Tel: 201-865-2065
Email: info@dayspaassociation.com
http://www.dayspaassociation.com

For more information on the spa industry, contact
International SPA Association
2365 Harrodsburg Road, Suite A325
Lexington, KY 40504-3335
Tel: 888-651-4772
Email: ispa@ispastaff.com
http://www.experienceispa.com

For information on accredited cosmetology schools and financial aid, contact
National Accrediting Commission of Cosmetology Arts and Sciences
4401 Ford Avenue, Suite 1300
Alexandria, VA 22302-1432
Tel: 703-600-7600
http://www.naccas.org

INTERVIEW

Jeremy McCarthy is the corporate director of development and marketing for spas at Starwood Hotels & Resorts. He discussed his career and the spa industry with the editors of Careers in Focus: Cosmetology.

Q. How long have you worked in the industry?

A. I have worked almost 18 years in the spa industry—mainly working in resort spa locations (including 14 years with Four Seasons, opening and operating luxury spas).

Q. Tell us about your job.

A. I currently work at Starwood Hotels & Resorts. My primary responsibility is to develop brand concepts for spas that fit into the brands of our hotels and then give them consulting and guidance to ensure that they are successful.

Q. Why did you decide to pursue a career in the spa/hospitality industry?

A. I came from a fitness background. I was a personal trainer and martial arts instructor, and when I opened my first spa, I was excited primarily because it included a small fitness center. I enjoyed it, but when I suggested that I wanted to continue developing spas I was told by my superiors that spas were just a fad and I should move into other areas of the hotel in order to develop my career. The other areas of the hotel did not interest me as much, so I just figured I would work in spas until something better came along. Nothing is better!

Q. What do you like most and least about your job?

A. I like the fact that we are impacting people's lives in a unique way. Our mission is to make people feel better—a great goal to accomplish every day. I also think that we impact the lives of our employees by teaching them how to take care of people in a special way. Whether they stay in the spa business or not, the skills they will learn will help them in any business endeavor they pursue and with any personal relationships they have.

    The spa business can be tough. I often feel like the spa staff has to absorb the stress of everyone who walks in the door. We take the stress on so our customers don't have to. My favorite parts of the job come from working with people. My least favorites are the administrative paperwork, inventories, ordering, etc. that come with running a business.

Q. What advice would you give to high school students who are interested in working in spas in the hospitality/resort industry?

A. It is a great career path in an increasingly competitive market. You have to have passion for what you do—that will push you to excel in spite of rising competition.

Experience is the great educator. Seek out experiences that will give you a well-rounded education on diverse aspects of the industry. Then find where your passion is the most powerful and specialize in that area.

Q. What is the future employment outlook for spa workers in the hotel industry, as well as the field in general?

A. Talented professionals have been hard to come by and, because of that, those who are available have been in high demand. Because of this, many people are drawn to the industry, so it is getting more competitive. It is also getting more divergent with different types of spas popping up everywhere. Medical spas are the largest growth segment in the industry, and I would anticipate more and more segmentation in the future. This gives professionals an opportunity to specialize in niche segments and experience career success in a unique way.

Index